HIGH STICK

HIGH STICK

By *Ted Green*

with *Al Hirshberg*

Illustrated with photographs

DODD, MEAD & COMPANY • NEW YORK

Copyright © 1971 by Al Hirshberg and Ted Green

All rights reserved

No part of this book may be reproduced in any form without permission in writing from the publisher

ISBN: 0-396-06427-2
Library of Congress Catalog Card Number: 77-179695

Printed in the United States of America
by The Cornwall Press, Inc., Cornwall, N. Y.

To Pat

Editor's Foreword

In 40 years of writing, mostly on sports, I have worked with many athletes. I never see them as stars, semi-stars, or would-be stars; but simply as people, who, in common with the rest of us, share many of the same emotions, problems, and moods. Some of these people I have found very hard to work with; others, easy. Even the simple act of talking into a microphone while taping with a collaborator may lead to occasional abrasiveness.

I have worked with some people who made every taping session an ordeal, who cancelled one date after another, or who promised to appear and didn't. Others had no real story to tell. But I have also worked with people who were both considerate and cooperative, and who had an outstanding story to tell.

Ted Green was one of these. A fine man, a devoted husband and father, a star of his profession, he suffered an injury so agonizing that it would have left a lesser man permanently handicapped. But within a year he was back in action as a Boston Bruin defenseman.

Throughout our association he never missed an appointment, never showed impatience, never withheld a memory no matter how painful to recall. And his lovely wife, Pat, assisted in every way possible. This is her story, too. She had a vital, active role in her husband's amazing comeback.

For me, this was not just a hockey story, nor just a sport story, but an inspirational family story—the research and recording of which has been one of the most memorable experiences of my career.

This is my 35th book. Its literary quality is not for me to judge. But the story and the people who made it possible have given me a professional satisfaction and a personal pleasure far beyond any ability of mine to express in words.

—AL HIRSHBERG

Boston, August 1971

HIGH STICK

Chapter / 1

December 2, 1970. As I skated out to my right defense position for the Boston Bruins in the packed Chicago Stadium, I was thinking, *I wonder if this game will be better? I can't be sure. Here we are, already halfway through the season, and I still don't want to be here. I don't like the nervous feeling I get when I go on the ice. I don't like thinking the way I'm thinking, or the way my hands sweat and my knees shake. I don't like not being able to do the job as I want to do it. My doctors and teammates tell me to forget these things—just think about playing hockey. It's so easy for them to say, so hard for me to do. I can't forget that easily—the nightmare is always there and I can't stop it.*

I looked over at my defense partner, Don Awrey. We had just gone out to relieve Dallas Smith and Bobby Orr, a tough act to follow. Who can do the things Orr can do?

Who can stop marveling at the way this kid makes all the right moves at the right times in the right places? I couldn't even have done them before Wayne Maki of the St. Louis Blues nearly killed me in September 1969. And now—

Now? So many nows—every game another now. Every game a little bit of extra hell. A question mark. A miracle. I could imagine what everyone in those big crowds that followed us around the circuit and packed the Boston Garden when we played at home was thinking: *What will he do right? How much will he do wrong? He can't be the Terrible Teddy Green we remember. He can't do the things he used to do. They say he makes mistakes he never made before. They say he no longer has any inclination to fight. He wears a helmet. Whoever thought Terrible Teddy Green would need protection on his head or anywhere else? Or want it?*

Terrible Teddy Green. The tough guy of the National Hockey League. That was the reputation I had before Maki bashed in my skull with his stick during an exhibition game in Ottawa. I didn't like the name or the reputation. I played hockey hard, and sure I hit because it was my job to hit. In my younger days maybe I went out of my way to find a fight, but not later. Two, three years before Maki hit me, I had stopped being Terrible Teddy Green. I held my ground, I battled for puck control, I hit back when I got hit. But that was to protect my part of the ice, my goalie, my partner, and myself.

And when I had the puck, I bulled my way down the ice with it—passing and taking passes, fighting across the blue line and through opposing defensemen. And I was respected. *Leave Ted Green alone and you'll be OK. Just don't start anything with him, not unless you want to get into trouble.*

That's the way it had been, but not now. Physically, I was in as good shape as ever—maybe a little better. But as Coach Tom Johnson sent me on the ice that night in Chicago, I got that awful feeling of inadequacy which engulfed me all during the early season. I wasn't afraid—just unsure of myself. And in the NHL you can't be unsure of yourself. If there's one thing you need more than anything else, it's confidence. You're better than the other guy and you know it. Only I wasn't sure. That doubt was killing me, killing my game, making me wonder what I was doing out on the ice.

I wish I could express the feeling. Maybe one way is to describe what happened in a November game we'd lost to Oakland a few weeks before. I don't want to take anything away from the Seals' play, because they were hot that Sunday night, but we had no business losing to an expansion team at home. I lost that game—I'm sure I did, and nobody can convince me otherwise. It was tied 1–1 in the third period when one of the Seals dumped the puck in on my side. Ordinarily this would have been no problem. I might have started up ice with it. Or, if a man were right on me and Awrey was free, I might have passed it across to Don. Or, if I got really tangled up with my opponent, I might have battled him to the boards to freeze the puck and force a faceoff.

I didn't do any of these things. In fact, I'm not sure what I did. All I know is that one minute I had control of the puck, and the next instant I didn't. One of the Seals' guys just swooped down, stole it right from under me, and with nobody in front of the net but our goalie, Eddie Johnston, slammed it home for a 2–1 win for them. Johnston didn't have a chance.

If I were the coach, I would have yanked me out right away. But Tom Johnson, a former defense partner of mine on the Bruins, kept me in for a few more minutes to save me further embarrassment. Johnson, who treated me with understanding and consideration almost all year, didn't fool me, or the crowd either. I didn't lose the puck in a wild scramble, with a lot of guys fighting for it. If somebody makes a mistake in a situation like that, it can't really be pinpointed. But my mistake was obvious to everyone at Boston Garden. I was all alone out there, holding the puck on my stick and obviously in control of it. When I lost control, a spectator had to be blind or looking the other way to miss it.

Maybe I was imagining things, but I could hear the crowd murmuring that night, too: *He lost the puck. . . . He never did it that way before. . . . Teddy Green hasn't got it anymore. . . . Give him "A" for effort, but he just isn't the hockey player he was. . . .*

And that night, as on many other nights, I wasn't my old self. Rarely are games so apparently lost by one man. When I skated off the ice after my turn with Awrey, my head was down and I prayed somebody would get that goal back in time for us to save at least a tie. I felt pats on the back—teammates, people behind the bench, maybe Tom Johnson or a trainer. They were friendly pats, to let me know that even if we lost on account of my blunder, they all understood.

That was the trouble. I needed understanding, but not that kind of understanding. I was fighting my way back, trying to jump from near death back into the NHL. I was desperately anxious to do it right, terribly aware that every eye was on me. And here, in front of nearly 15,000 people, I had blown a goal, and with it a game.

Later, in the dressing room, the guys came over with a word or two of encouragement. My buddy, Eddie Johnston, telling me it wasn't my fault. Derek "Turk" Sanderson and Phil Esposito, whose lockers are near mine, saying everybody makes mistakes—Turk, in fact, calling hockey a game of mistakes, which I suppose it is. Bobby Orr coming over to tell me not to blame myself. Eddie Westfall, who broke into the Bruins with me, saying something to make me feel better. I don't think a single player didn't stop by as I sat staring, unseeing, into my locker.

And still later, long after I showered and dressed for the street, there was Pat, my wife, who never missed a home game, never let a chance go by to buck me up, never admitted to herself or anyone else that anything that went wrong was my fault, waiting at the door for me. I looked at her, and with tears in my eyes I just raised my hands in a gesture of frustration.

Neither of us said anything until we were in the car heading home to Lynnfield, on Boston's North Shore. Then I muttered, "I lost it."

"You didn't lose it, Ted," Pat said emphatically. "No one man loses a game."

"I lost this one."

"You made a mistake. Everybody makes mistakes."

"They were all saying the same things in the locker room," I said. "But they knew—they all knew. And you know. If I had kept control of that puck, we wouldn't have lost the game. But it slipped away from me."

"Don't think about that, Ted. It's happened before and it will happen again."

"That's it, honey," I said. "It hasn't happened before— not for years, not since I was a kid. I never made mistakes like that."

"You're looking for miracles," she said. "You've made miracles already. Every doctor, coach, trainer—everyone who's helped—said you wouldn't even be on skates until January. You were on skates the day the training season opened, less than a year after you were hurt. And you've been playing in the fastest hockey league in the world since the season started."

"And I cost us a game."

We talked all the way home, with Pat commiserating and me blaming myself. Nobody was kidding me. I lost that hockey game. Me, Teddy Green. And I lost it because I couldn't control the puck. Teddy Green—Terrible Teddy Green, if you insist—had the puck laid right on his stick and then lost it.

As I stood out on the ice in Chicago, memories of that Oakland loss and of all those early games flashed through my mind. Obvious mistakes, not always as costly, but just as obvious—passing the puck to an opponent, letting it slip away when it was right on my stick, losing it on the boards after I had beaten my man to it, not freezing it solidly enough for a faceoff, getting in the way of the goalie instead of protecting him, failing to carry the puck because I didn't trust myself to keep it.

And not fighting. Maybe, in a way, that was the most upsetting. Despite my reputation, I hadn't been looking for fights even before I was hurt—I just never ran away from them. Now I was avoiding them, backtracking if one seemed to be coming my way. If I was lucky, I could divert a man into the corner, but I didn't fight him, didn't battle, didn't try to crash him into the boards, didn't swing at him, grab him, or do anything to get the puck away from him. I could almost hear the word getting around the league: *Go down Green's side. The poor guy can't do anything. He's helpless against a big rush. He doesn't get in the way anymore. He won't hit and he can't hurt.*

Even worse than that were those other words going

through the league: *Don't go after Green. Don't try to hurt him. He's been hurt enough. He's making a game attempt to do the impossible. Don't hit him unless you have to—and then don't hit him hard. He's a good guy and he deserves every break.* Pity. Compassion. Sympathy. That was the most horrible thing. I didn't want that—I wanted to earn my way back, to have the respect of my opponents the way it was before I got hurt. Then they didn't dare start a fight. Now they didn't want to. I had been too badly hurt. Nobody had the heart or the inclination to hurt me again.

The brain damage had all been on the right side of my head, which controls nerves on the left side—and I'm left-handed. While recovering, I could skate, handle a stick, and carry a puck before I could write my name. When I was Terrible Teddy Green—even after that, but before Maki hit me—they all tried to stay away from my left side. I hit with my left hip or my left shoulder. I punched with my left hand. My left side was my strong side. And now, as guys came down the ice, they knew I couldn't—or wouldn't—use it.

I could not understand why. The doctor had assured me my left side was as strong as ever, the plastic coating over the hole in my head sturdier than the bone it had replaced. I didn't have to worry about it anymore. And yet I did. *Terrible Teddy Green worried? Why?* Perhaps "worry" is the wrong word. I didn't care about getting hit, nor did I turn my right side to catch a possible check and absorb the shock. It was more a loss of confidence and of timing than worry. My timing was so far off I couldn't have made a move either way to check an oncoming opponent. I wasn't afraid, in the sense that I wanted to avoid fights. It was really more a matter of avoiding cheap penalties. Every minute of ice time I got in a game was precious, and you get no ice time while serving a penalty. If one were slapped on me I wanted it to be for a real fight, not some small rule infraction.

Before every game I gave myself pep talks: *Confidence—that's the key—confidence—in this game you can't survive without it.* And it was bothering me when, after jumping the boards in front of our bench that early December night in Chicago, I moved into the spot Orr always filled so well.

If I can only get totally absorbed in the game. If I can only forget myself and close my mind to everything except hockey. Then I can do it. Then I can hit hard and well, and carry my share of the load. Except I can't forget—I can't forget that terrible night in Ottawa and the awful weeks and months that followed. Maybe this time. Maybe this game. Maybe something will happen to make me the hockey player I was before. I've got it all back physically. It's the mental block I have to lick.

There was another problem—an odd one, in a way. The Bruins were so strong, so much the class of the league, that they often ran away with a game, sometimes winning by three or four goals. When we were that hot, that far ahead, that overwhelming, it was doubly hard for me to get fired up. The close games, the ones we were in danger of losing, were the kind I needed, because then I sometimes could lose myself in hockey, stop thinking about myself and concentrate more on the business at hand.

While this hurt me in one way, it helped in another. Because we were so strong—we had won the Stanley Cup the previous season—I got more ice time than I would have on a losing club. My teammates could cover for me when I made a mistake. I could be carried as a weak spot—which I was the first few months of the season—because the rest of the team was so great. A losing club couldn't stand a weak spot, and on a losing club I would have spent much more time on the bench. The strength of the Bruins was a big break for me, as was Coach Tom Johnson's attitude. By pairing me with Awrey he had a strong man backing me up. And by using me as much as he did, he gave me ice time I so badly needed to regain my form. That was one thing I had to have—playing in championship games against big-league opposition.

On that December night at the Chicago Stadium, I still wasn't myself. I had shown an occasional flash, but I hadn't got into a single fight, hadn't thrown a punch, hadn't bulled my way past anybody. I had made only a few good checks and sometimes an accurate pass—outside of my skating, my passing was really the first thing that came back—but I needed confidence, and I didn't have it yet.

I couldn't understand why. Before games, I had no trouble psyching myself up. Every professional athlete has to do that in his own way. Some guys want to be left alone, to think, to figure the opposition and how it should be handled, to work up to a high pitch of excitement and anticipation, even to generate a sort of ersatz hate for everyone on the other team. In the NHL, your best friend off the ice is your worst enemy when you play against him. Even Phil Esposito, who is very close to his brother, Tony, the Chicago goalie, has to forget all that when we play the Hawks. On those nights, it's not one Esposito against the other—it's the great high-scoring Bruins' center against the great Black Hawks' goalie. Blood may be thicker than water, but in pro hockey, uniforms are thicker than blood.

Other guys psych themselves by kidding around—making wisecracks, telling foolish little stories, talking to anyone who'll listen. Some guys go into the trainers' room and lie down to rest. Some talk about sports or interests other than hockey—baseball, football, boxing, basketball, movies, television, women, anything that comes to mind. Some talk to newspapermen or other locker-room visitors.

I like to be left alone—I always have. I guess maybe I appear to be brooding. I'm not, but it has the same effect on outsiders. I could psych myself just as well after Maki hurt me as before. The difference came when I skated out on the ice. All the psyching in the world couldn't keep me calm and confident, not in those early months of the 1970–

71 season. I shook, I worried, I wondered. Sometimes I felt that way all evening. Other times I got over it after two or three turns on the ice. But I couldn't get rid of it altogether, and that worried me more than anything.

It was this feeling—and, I'm sure, only this feeling—that gave me a tendency to lose shots I should have blocked. This is one of a defenseman's prime jobs, and I wasn't doing it as often as I should. When I did do it, I felt good because then I knew I was functioning properly. But blocking shots shouldn't have made me so happy. In the old days, it was second nature. Now it had become the exception.

Why? I didn't know. It certainly wasn't fear of the puck. I have been hit by flying pucks a million times. When you block a shot, you're being hit. You take it on your shin pads, or your body, or your skates. Or maybe you catch it with one hand and knock it down in front of you so you can keep control of it. Or, if you're lucky, you'll block it with your stick, and then you don't feel anything at all. But whatever you feel, it isn't bad pain. I've always had a high tolerance for pain. I don't mind bruises or bumps—hell, they're part of the game.

I would sit in front of my locker after games and go over all the shots I hadn't blocked. I couldn't figure out what I was doing wrong, and why. I knew it wasn't a physical problem, any more than my not getting into fights was. It was totally mental. Something stopped me from doing the right thing. I wanted to know what it was, and when at first I couldn't find out, it really bugged me.

There were times Tom Johnson didn't have confidence in me, times he couldn't help but make it obvious. I'd pull some horrible bloop just when it looked as if I were getting it all back, and Tom might say, "Ted, rest the next turn," or, "Ted, you're tired. I'm going to let you sit out a while." Sometimes he didn't say anything—just put somebody else in with Awrey. Once, near midseason, I asked him for more ice time, and he gave it to me. But he didn't have the confidence coaches used to have in me, and I couldn't say I blamed him. If I were a coach and had a defenseman out there who *might* block a shot, or *might* freeze the puck, or *might* push an opponent away, or *might* make a good pass, or *might* take the puck down the ice, I wouldn't have much confidence in him either. Too many "mights." With games on the line, you can go along with a guy like that just so long, then you have to make a move.

Since Tom and I understood each other, there were rarely any problems between us. As a matter of fact, we had a lot in common. While we were defense mates, Tom, who for 15 years was an NHL standout, first with the Montreal Canadiens and then with us, was knocked out of hockey by Wayne Maki's brother, Chico, who has been with the Hawks all through his career. When Chico slicked Tom in the back of the legs with his skates and severed a nerve, that was the end of Tom's career.

My own feeling about Wayne Maki is zero. He was with

Vancouver in the 1970–71 season, and every time we played the Canucks, people wondered what would happen if Maki and I collided. We didn't. If he hadn't stayed away from me, I'd have stayed away from him. I wanted—and want—no part of that guy. He's apparently a nut with his stick, because even after he cooled me with it he couldn't control his urge to use it on people. As recently as the 1970–71 season, he was set down for five games for belting somebody with it.

Don't get me wrong—I'm not afraid of Maki. I just don't want to have anything to do with him. Maybe he feels the same way. The few times we were on the ice together we hardly ever went near each other. Frankly, if I saw him coming at me, I'd go the other way. Maybe I'm afraid of myself, of what I might do to the guy. All I know is, the less I see of him the better.

Funny, in all these early games, right up to the one in Chicago on December 2, the same thoughts flashed through my head. That was one of the problems. I was thinking too much. What made me an NHL star were things I did without thinking. The moves were natural, a part of me. I didn't have to think, *I'm going to hit this guy*—I just hit him. I didn't have to think, *I'm going to block the puck*—I just blocked it.

Now everything was mental. It was a problem I had to lick. If I didn't, it would lick me. After all I had gone through to get into shape to return to the NHL, I *couldn't* let overthinking get the better of me. Something had to happen to help me conquer it—or maybe, without conscious thought, I could make something happen.

For this reason the December 2 game in Chicago was so important. That was the night something in me opened up and let all the gremlins out. That was the night I became the old Teddy Green, the Teddy Green I had been, the Teddy Green I wanted to be again. I made mistakes in later games, and once in a while I still got the shakes, but on December 2, I turned the corner and started moving in the right direction. That was the night my confidence returned. I knew for sure I was going to make it, after all.

It was a rough game, with a lot of pushing and elbowing and scrambling—one of those games you know will blow sky-high sooner or later. About halfway through the second period, when Don Awrey got into a fight with one of the Black Hawk players, I skated over to give him a hand. I definitely wasn't looking for a fight—all I wanted to do was break up this one. As I approached the two guys battling near the boards on the left side of our defensive zone, Dan Maloney, a 20-year-old Chicago rookie who stands six feet and weighs about 200 pounds, grabbed Awrey from behind and started punching him. In the short time Maloney had been in the league, we'd learned he was a "sucker" puncher—somebody who makes a specialty of surprising an opponent by hitting him when he's not looking or is busy fighting somebody else, as Awrey was.

That Don had been covering for me all year, probably doing more for me than anyone else on the ice because he was my partner, was not nearly as important to me as the fact he was a teammate in trouble. He needed help, and you help a teammate any time you can. That's the code of our business.

My original reason for going over to where Awrey was fighting was to help him, and maybe Maloney's reason for suckering him was to help a Chicago player. In any event, Maloney had already hit Awrey and was trying to hold him from behind when I got there. By then, all I wanted to do was get Maloney—get the kid off Awrey's back so Don could keep swinging, or at least protect himself. I dropped my stick and gloves and started hauling Maloney off Awrey. As I pinned his arms and pulled him away, Maloney said, "Let go, I'm not going to hit you."

Knowing his tendencies, I wasn't going to fall for that without being ready to protect myself—in fact, I didn't want to fight at all because I still wasn't sure of myself. But since he was now clear of Awrey, I let him go, and, sure enough, he tried to sucker me. I ducked, and his punch went over my shoulder and by my head. My helmet slipped down over my face, scratching my nose, and I blew up. While I yanked at the helmet, Maloney tried to sucker me again, and again he missed. By the time I was rid of that damn helmet, instinct took over and I could swing freely. I did it naturally—left-handed. I nailed him with four good lefts in a row, hitting him so hard that he started sliding down the side boards onto the ice. Somebody had to pull me off before I stopped swinging. The way I was hitting the kid, I'd have knocked him cold. As it was, I dazed him, and he had to go to the dressing room when most of us drew penalties.

I guess I wasn't even thinking as I picked up my gloves and stick and skated over to the penalty box. But I felt a sudden warmth, the comfort that comes when something very good happens.

I felt these things rather than thinking them. I was grinning, almost laughing, as I served my time in the penalty box. And I grinned still more after getting out when I went over to our bench, where the guys were yelling and laughing and throwing friendly punches at me.

Not until then did I realize the little finger on my left hand hurt like hell. This was curious, because one of the first effects of my skull fracture had been paralysis of my left side, including numbness in my hands and fingers. Actually, even that long after the injury, I couldn't write easily or clearly, and—as is still the case—I had no feeling in the tips of the fingers of my left hand. I looked down and saw the little finger was crooked. I tried to move it and almost yelled with pain.

Then I smiled—smiled like a crazy man. *God, I thought, I broke my finger throwing punches. Imagine, I belted him so hard I broke my finger—and on my left hand!* I studied my hand again. Except for the little finger, it was fine. I found Frosty Foristall, our assistant trainer, and eased over to him.

"My finger's sore," I said. "I've got to keep playing tonight, so fix it up."

"It looks broken," Frosty said.

"It probably is," I said. "Do something."

Frosty quickly made a little mold for a temporary splint, while I thought, *I can use my left—I can use my left—I can use my left.* The words rang in my mind as Frosty worked so fast I don't think I missed a turn on the ice. When Tom Johnson gave the word, I jumped the boards with Awrey, ready for anything.

I played the rest of the game with that broken finger, and not only did I not worry about what might happen, I played exceptionally well. Nothing much happened, really. The Hawks had learned something, too, and they left me alone. When the puck came into my zone, nobody came barreling hard after it the way everyone had before. Nobody wanted to tangle with me, or start a fight, or try to belt me around. *They're not afraid of hurting me anymore,* I thought. *They're afraid of my hurting them.*

We lost the game, which didn't make me happy, but my heart was singing when it was over. They could call me Terrible Teddy Green all they wanted to now. It was just an incident, but what an incident! It taught me to feel what everyone, including the doctors who checked me from time to time, had been telling me right along—my left side was strong, and I could expose it to anything I had ever exposed it to before, and it would hold up.

In the locker room later, Frosty and Dan Canney, our

head trainer, made a removable metal splint, while guys came in and out, joking and patting my back and saying things like, "What the hell's a broken finger?" Despite the loss, they were happy for me. They knew I had found something I'd been looking for all year—myself, the old Teddy Green.

Chapter / 2

September 21, 1969. Ottawa, clean and beautiful, glistened beneath a warm sun that streamed through the windows of my hotel room as I awoke on that Sunday morning. It was a lovely day, a lovely town, a lovely place to be at that time of year. It was good to be alive, to go to Mass and give thanks to God for my wife and children and parents, and for the talent to play hockey which He had blessed me with.

At peace with the world, I strolled with Turk Sanderson past the spacious Chateau Laurier Hotel and through the wide greenery of Parliament Park, its old, impressive government buildings towering majestically over acres of grass extending the entire seven or eight blocks between the Chateau and the sprawling Ottawa General Hospital. The grounds looked like a huge, flat, marvelously well-kept golf course that was all fairway and no greens. Although this was my ninth season with the Bruins and my eleventh in professional hockey, I had never seen Ottawa, which is slightly off the beaten paths between NHL cities and is almost 300 miles from our training camp in London, Ontario.

I don't remember much of the conversation with Turk, except that I remarked how foolish it was to go all out in such things as the pre-season exhibition games we had to play, and that I didn't intend to do so. We were in Ottawa for a game that night against the St. Louis Blues, who trained there. The preceding night we had played an exhibition with the Canadiens in Montreal. I never liked exhibition games because of the chances of getting hurt before the regular season started. Because of injuries or contract disputes, I doubt if I played more than half a dozen exhibition games the previous five years. I kept myself in condition during the off-season at my home in St. Boniface, just outside Winnipeg, Manitoba. The only reason I cared about training at all after I made the club was to get into skating shape, which never took more than a few weeks.

I had played in the Canadiens' game on this trip and was scheduled to play again that night against the Blues. I wasn't happy about it and told Sanderson so, but I needed the work. Turk agreed with me, saying something to the effect that if he got hurt he hoped it wouldn't be in an exhibition, but in a game that counted. He wasn't even going to dress for the Blues game because he and the

Bruins hadn't yet come to terms. I guess I told him I thought he was lucky—that I'd rather be in the stands with him for a game like this than out on the ice.

I remember being very pleased because, after a summer of doubt and some hassling over my contract, everything had just been settled. Only a few days before, Charlie Mulcahy, the Bruins' lawyer, and I had reached an agreement. I'd had a great year the season before—I made the second NHL all-star team—and now I was getting a new three-year contract at a nice raise in salary. The only reason I hadn't actually signed was that a few clauses which had been at issue were in the process of being changed on paper in Boston. All I had was a handshake, but with the Bruins that was all I needed. The signing would come in due time.

After meandering through the park for an hour or so, Turk and I went back to the hotel. I loafed around with the guys, ate, and slept a little before going with the team to the arena in the city's new Civic Center. This must be one of the most unique sports complexes in the world because of its all-embracing yet space-saving layout. The arena where we would play the Blues holds about 10,000 people and is the home of the Ottawa 67's, a Junior A team in the Ontario Hockey League. Built right on the arena roof is one side of the stands overlooking the field where the Ottawa Rough Riders of the Canadian Football League play their home games. It holds 15,000 people, more than half the 28,000 capacity of the stadium. The rest of the stands are on the opposite side of the field. The arena and field are part of a huge setup for professional and amateur sports, which includes facilities for individual and team games as well.

We arrived there a couple of hours before the game, our usual procedure, and horsed around in the locker room before changing into uniforms. There is a standing joke on the club about me looking Jewish, and every once in a while the guys call me "Abie." This is one of the ways we all loosen up—yelling foolish names at each other. Anyway, somebody said this was a Jewish holiday and asked me if I was going to play that night. If Sandy Koufax could take a Jewish holiday off, why couldn't I? While the guys were kidding me, Milt Schmidt, our general manager, walked into the dressing room. When I saw him, I handed him my skates and said, "I can't play tonight."

"What the hell's wrong with you?" he said.

"It's a Jewish holiday."

It broke up the whole locker room. The guys were still laughing about it when we went out to the ice for our pregame workout. Until then I had done very little skating—I think it was only my third time on the ice, including the Canadiens exhibition game the night before. The place was full, a solid sellout. I looked up in the stands and spotted Turk with goalie Eddie Johnston, who was also in street clothes, since Gerry Cheevers was in the nets for us that night. I didn't pay much attention to the Blues. They had guys I knew, and a lot I didn't. Like most expansion clubs, there were a flock of rookies. Those kids usually are the ones to watch because they play harder than veterans in pre-season exhibition games. Fighting for jobs, they have to make an impression or they get lost in the shuffle.

There was a slight mist over the ice, as there always is on a warm day. It's caused by the combination of heat outside and cold inside, and the longer you play, the softer the ice becomes. The first 12 minutes of the game went by without much happening. It was a dull game, with no checking, no scoring, no fighting, no nothing.

Around the twelfth or thirteenth minute, while I was guarding the right side of our defensive zone, somebody shot the puck over our blue line and followed it in. I didn't even notice who it was—just a blue uniform. Later I discovered it was Wayne Maki, a left wing, but I didn't know that then. He had been up and down in the league, first with the Chicago Black Hawks, now with the Blues, and he was one of the kids fighting for a regular job. I didn't recognize him—in fact, the only time I'd ever played against him had been when he took one turn on the ice against us while he was a Hawk. I wasn't particularly concerned about him.

As I trapped the puck behind the net, the kid hit me from behind, and I got a little ticked off, as I always do when that happens. But my first obligation was to clear the puck. I kicked it with my skate up to my stick, and shot it out around the boards to our right wing. Then I turned to take care of the guy who hit me. By that time we'd both moved in front and a little to the left of our net. I reached out with my gloved left hand and shoved Maki in the face. He went down by the side of the net. Figuring that was the end of that, I turned away, but then Maki speared me in the abdomen. Spearing, which is shoving the blade of your stick into a guy, is a filthy trick, because if you get him in an unprotected spot he can be badly hurt. That and butt-ending (hitting an opponent with the butt of your stick) are dangerous, and only a guy who is naturally mean or crazy will do it.

Anyhow, where at first I had just been annoyed, now I was sore as hell, and I hit Maki with my stick just below the shoulder at the bicep, knocking him off balance and, I think, down on one knee. I say "I think" because I'm really not sure, and I wouldn't know at all what happened next except from pictures and from what I was told. Seeing Maki on the ice is the last clear memory I have. My last thought was, *Well, I guess that'll straighten him out,* and, again, I turned to skate away.

The next thing I knew, I was lying on my stomach with my head turning violently. I remember trying to stop it from moving, but I couldn't because I had no control over it. It was whipping back and forth, and everything else that followed is vague in my memory—little snatches of action, dim pictures of guys around me. I didn't know what hit me, didn't remember anything hitting me, didn't feel a damn thing—no pain, nothing except this violent head movement I couldn't stop.

I don't remember going down and I don't remember getting up. Everything was hazy because my eyes were full of water and things were very, very blurry. I still felt no pain, didn't see or feel any blood, didn't know what was happening at all. I was just in a complete fog, terribly dazed, and yelling something—I don't know what. And I remember that nothing came out clearly. I couldn't control my speech. I saw a haze of players, but the only one I remember was Bobby Orr, who had been on the bench and was now on the ice. Dan Canney, our trainer, and somebody else (I found out later it was Phil Esposito) were trying to lead me off the ice, but I tried to push them away. I don't remember how I got off, who led me, where I went, what I did. And I didn't know what had happened, where I had been hit, what I had been hit with, how badly I was hurt. It was the only time in my career I ever got hit without seeing the blow coming—the only time I turned away thinking a fight was over when it wasn't.

". . . I saw the two guys pushing each other around, but I didn't think anything of it," Canney said later. "That sort of thing happens all the time in a game. I turned away for a second, then turned back just in time to see Maki hit Ted with his stick. Bobby Orr, sitting in front of me, jumped the boards, saying something about going after Maki. I followed him because I knew Ted was badly hurt. He went down with his knees buckling, and then his head kept thrashing around. Even as I was jumping the boards, I could see his eyes glazed and staring oddly. I got to him as fast as I could, but I was still 20 feet away when he stood up under his own power. Phil was holding him by the arm and Ted was mumbling almost incoherently. The only blood I saw was from a small cut on the right side of his scalp.

"'Canney,' he muttered thickly, 'I'm gonna get that guy.'

"'Come on, Teddy, you're cut,' I said. 'Let's go in and get you fixed up. Bobby's taking care of Maki. You'll get a shot at him later.'

"He kept muttering, his speech so garbled I thought he had broken his jaw. The head wound seemed slight. But I knew Ted was in serious trouble. When I tried to grab him, he pulled away from me, so I took him by the seat of the pants, and, with Phil holding him on the other side, we finally got him off the ice."

". . . My first thought was to get Maki," Orr said, "but by the time I got across the ice, he was swinging his stick while the Blues were trying to get him out of there. Then I went over to Teddy, who was stumbling around on his feet. I had no idea how badly hurt he was. I just said, 'Take it easy,' and stood and watched Dan and Phil lead him off."

". . . I was at the red line, right at center ice, when the fight started," Esposito recalled. "They were sparring over in the corner near the Bruins' goal when Maki went down on one knee. He got right up and hit Greenie over the head with the hardest part of his stick—at the bend where the shaft joins the blade. Greenie was down when I reached him, and he looked awful. When he got up his voice was fuzzy and he kept saying something like, 'I'm gonna get that sonofabitch. I'll kill him—I'll kill him.' His eyes were glassy, and spit or something was coming out of his mouth, which was all twisted on the left side. He looked so bad I was scared to death. I took him by the left side, and when Dan came he tried to take his right. But Greenie kept pulling away from him and telling us to leave him alone so he could get Maki. Canney was saying, 'It's all right, Teddy—it's all right—' but we both knew damn well it wasn't all right. We finally got Greenie off. I just went as far as the boards, and Dan took him from there.

"When I started back, Maki was taking wild swipes with his stick to keep us away from him. I don't blame him for being scared. I guess he thought we really would kill him. We were all trying to get at him until the Blues pulled him off the ice. Later I was thrown out for heckling the referee. I told him he was calling a lousy game and should have stopped the fight. I guess I called him a few names, and he gave me a ten-minute misconduct. I didn't give a damn. All I could think of was that funny look in Greenie's eyes, and the funny way he was talking."

". . . I was around the blue line trying to figure out why Teddy hadn't moved up with me when we got the puck,"

Awrey said. "Bill Plager of the Blues met me there and we got into a little hassle—just one of those shoving matches. My back was to our net and Bill was facing it when he grabbed me. All of a sudden he let go and said, 'Jeez, Greenie's hurt bad. Go help him.' I turned around, and even from where I was I could see Teddy's eyes staring, and I thought, *My God, what is it?* I started skating toward him, but Espi and Dan were already leading him to the boards. The whole thing happened in a flash."

". . . It started like a routine stick fight," Gerry Cheevers said. "Then Maki speared Teddy, and Teddy hit him on the shoulder. I stayed away because I knew Teddy could handle him. But then Maki whacked him right on the head with his stick. It was a direct hit. One of the officials was there, but he couldn't do anything alone. He wouldn't have been very bright staying in the middle, because one referee can't handle two hockey players. As soon as Teddy fell, I went after Maki, but I couldn't move fast with those heavy pads and the big stick and all. Even though he slowed up to swing his stick, Maki was at the Blues' bench before I caught up with him. When I looked back, Teddy was off the ice."

". . . I was standing in a corner of the stands in plain view of the whole thing, about 15 feet away from it," Sanderson said. "Maki had the puck, coming down the right side. As he came near the faceoff circle by the Bruins' net, he tried to lean into Green to cut the corner. Green hit him on the side of the face and Maki went down. Maki, on his knees, speared Green in the stomach—a two-handed spear that stopped Greenie just long enough to give Maki time to get up. After Green recovered, he slashed Maki across the shoulder. Then they fenced for a second, the referee put up his hands, and Green turned his head away, apparently thinking the fight was over. Maki went up on his toes and brought the stick right down on Green's head. Greenie dropped and rolled, and even from where I was you could see the whites of his eyes."

". . . Our bench was about halfway up the ice between the two goals, on the opposite side from where the incident occurred," Eddie Westfall said. "That was diagonally down and across the ice as we looked to the left. I jumped off the bench—I guess we all did—and headed for Teddy, but Dan and Espi were already starting to take him off the ice. I didn't try to talk to him because he appeared to be in a state of shock. I've seen people in shock—the glazed look, the twitching, the twisted face. That's the way Teddy was."

". . . After Maki knocked Green down, I thought the whole Bruins' team would go nuts," said Howard Darwin, owner of the 67's, who saw the game. "They poured off their bench heading for Maki, but somebody hustled him into one of the rooms. He got dressed, and later I saw him watching the game in street clothes from upstairs."

I don't remember leaving the ice or how I got into one of the rooms beneath the arena stands. I have a vague recollection of sitting on a table trying to get my eyes to focus properly. There were a lot of people milling around, but few I recognized. One was Frosty Foristall, who seemed very agitated about something, and I think Eddie Johnston was in the room. I don't remember seeing Canney (the other guys call him "Dan," but I've called him "Canney" as long as I've known him). Still dazed, my eyes watery, my speech almost unintelligible, I wondered what all the excitement was about, because in those few minutes I really didn't think I was badly hurt. I kept grabbing Foristall's jacket and mumbling at him, but I don't know what I said. When I heard somebody mention a stretcher and an ambulance, I tried to yell, but the words didn't come out right. My tongue seemed all twisted up. A couple of doctors were there, and one told me to lie down so he could put a stitch in my scalp. When I did, it suddenly felt very, very good. The doctor worked on me for only a few seconds. Then I heard Frosty (or maybe it was Canney) screaming, apparently in an argument with somebody. I didn't know. I didn't care. I just lay there, kind of comfortable, wishing everybody would go away and leave me alone.

I remember somebody grabbing me and taking off my skates, pads, and shirt, but the rest of my equipment—pants, underclothing, shoulder pads, jockstrap—all stayed on. The next thing I knew, I was being moved, and I guess people thought I was unconscious, but I wasn't. My left hand felt tingly, and I remember a whole sea of faces, none of which I recognized.

After they lifted me into an ambulance, my hand seemed worse. The tingly feeling was replaced by numbness. I remember Frosty was with me, but I don't recall if we talked, or anything except being wheeled along a corridor, with walls, ceiling, and people speeding by because they were wheeling me so fast. I remember being taken into a brightly lit room and being put on a table, where nurses and guys trying to take the rest of my clothes off all seemed jumbled together.

Now my head was beginning to hurt like hell, and I remember getting mad at everybody for trying to strip me without damaging any of my equipment. This was ridiculous, because we rip that stuff off all the time when we have to—what the hell's the sense of trying to save a jock? I was trying to tell the nurse to cut everything off. My head was hurting and I wanted somebody to do something about it. The nurse didn't pay any attention, but kept trying to take that junk off as if it were a ballet skirt. Maybe she couldn't make out what I was saying. Or perhaps she didn't understand English, since this was a predominantly French hospital. Anyhow, somebody else came along and finally cut off the stuff and covered me up.

I must have passed out for a few minutes, because the next thing I remember was asking for the last rites of the church, and I remember the priest coming in. It was the first time I had ever asked for last rites, and I didn't know what to say and couldn't have made myself understood if I had known. I remember he told me not to try to talk, and I remember his touching my forehead and saying something I couldn't understand. He asked me questions, but I don't remember what they were—or maybe he asked me before he told me not to talk. It's all mixed up in my mind, except I must have finally realized that I was badly hurt.

Off and on, I remember crying. It was almost a reflex. I cried when I couldn't feel anything in my left hand, and when I couldn't control the left side of my face. I cried because my head hurt, and I cried because I didn't know if I was going to die when I wanted so badly to live, and I cried when I thought of Pat and my kids and my parents and my brothers.

I remember a pleasant young guy bending over me and smiling and asking me how I felt, and I remember him telling me he was Dr. Michael Richard. I remember asking him to phone Pat in St. Boniface. One of the things that kept flashing through my mind was how fast newspapers and radio and TV pick up news, and I didn't want her to find out about me that way. The doctor promised to call her, and said he'd see me shortly.

I remember being wheeled out and shooting up in an elevator and going into another room for X rays. That's quite distinct in my mind, because when they took one of the pictures of my head, they had it hanging over the edge of the table resting on a plate of some kind, which hurt something awful. I moaned and groaned and tried to tell them please to put my head back up because the pain was so bad. I think I heard someone ask for a bandage, so maybe I started bleeding again. Later, when they took me out of there, my head hurt worse than it had before.

Impressions kept flashing through my mind, but nothing was very distinct after that. I remember being in a room for a little while, and seeing a guy in green who looked familiar. He was smiling and asking me what kind of haircut I wanted—that he was going to shave my head and it wouldn't hurt. I muttered something, and that's the last thing I remember until the next morning.

". . . Ted was much easier to handle after I got him off the ice than before," said Canney. "And, although dazed, he seemed instinctively aware of what was going on. There's a corridor leading from the ice under the stands, with two corridors off it on the left and a long stairway between them. The Bruins dressed in a room off the first corridor, and Ted started turning in there. I told him we weren't going there, but to a room off the other corridor. When I noticed a wire stretched across the corridor we were in, I said, 'Be careful of that wire, Ted. It may be live'—and he stepped over it. We passed the stairway, turned down the second corridor, and went into the Blues' trainers' room down near the end. Ted walked the whole way on his skates, just leaning lightly on me for support, and then he sat on the table.

"The room was filling up fast. Eddie Johnston came in and Turk Sanderson was at the door. There were a couple of doctors, and a lot of other people milling around. One of the doctors got Ted to lie flat while he took the stitch in his scalp, and the other one pulled me aside and said, 'I guess he's OK.'

" 'What do you mean, OK?' I yelled. 'You're not just going to leave him like this, are you?'

" 'Why not?'

" 'Well,' I said, 'look at the way he's talking.'

" 'I thought all hockey players talk that way,' the guy said.

"Later, Teddy told me he thought he heard Frosty arguing with somebody in the dressing room, but I'm pretty sure he meant me. He just didn't remember seeing me there. Anyhow, after I finished yelling at one doctor, I went over to the other while Tom Woodcock, the Blues' trainer, stayed with Teddy to make sure he didn't fall off the table. As soon as I reached the doctor, he said, 'He's not right, is he?'

" 'No,' I said. 'There's something wrong. He's talking funny. Do you think he could have broken his jaw?'

" 'It's a good possibility.'

"The doctor went over, tested Ted's jaw, then came back and said, 'His jaw's all right, but I'm quite concerned. I think we'd better get him to the hospital immediately.' He and the other doctor talked, and I saw them both nodding in apparent agreement. Then Frosty came in and said, 'Dan, the game's started again.'

"'He's going to the hospital,' I said.

"'OK, I'll go with him,' Frosty said.

"Then I went back out to the ice."

"... I went over to the room with Turk," Johnston recalled. "He stood at the door while I went in. Teddy looked so terrible I nearly cried when I saw him. I didn't stay more than a few seconds. Then I went back to Turk and said, 'Don't go in there. It'll make you sick.'

"'Why?'

"'Because he looks so bad.'

"Then we heard somebody say, 'Get an ambulance. It looks like a skull fracture,' and we both had to hold back tears as we stood there."

"... When I got into the room, Teddy reached out and grabbed me," Foristall said. "And he said over and over, 'Frosty, make sure I walk out of here.'

"And over and over, even though I knew damn well he wouldn't, I said, 'Don't worry, Teddy, you'll walk out.'

"The doctors were talking together when I first got there. One came over to me and said, 'Be sure and tell them at the hospital I put a stitch in. It'll probably have to come out.' He turned to Teddy and said, 'Don't worry. It's just a small cut.'

"I took off Teddy's skates, and he held up his hands so I could get his shirt off over his head. While Teddy kept mumbling about walking out, I was trying to figure how we could get him on a stretcher without his raising hell. I happened to look up and see a couple of cops at the door just as the stretcher came, so I said, 'Teddy, we've got to carry you out on account of the police laws in this town.' I guess that did it because he didn't say a word as I took his shoulders and one of the doctors his feet, and we slid him onto the stretcher. The two cops took over then because they had to get him up those stairs to the street level where the ambulance was. I walked along, past Johnston and Sanderson and through a crowd of fans who lined both sides of the stairs and the lobby at the top. When they got him into the ambulance, I went in after him, and the two of us rode alone to the Ottawa General Hospital.

"Teddy reached out, grabbed my right hand with his left, and started squeezing. For a second his grip seemed firm, but then it began getting weaker, and he started crying. He wept all the way to the hospital, and was still holding my hand and crying when we got him into the emergency ward. Some interns and nurses were just standing there staring at him, and I said, 'He needs X rays right away.' Then, remembering what the doctor had said at the arena, I added, 'He's got one stitch in his head.' I looked down at Teddy's limp hand in mine, and, nearly crying myself, I took a towel and wiped his face. When nobody moved I got mad and yelled, 'What's going on? Somebody do something. He's badly hurt. Let's get going to X-ray.'

"Bad as he was, he had flashes of awareness of what was going on, even though he didn't remember them later.

When a doctor came in and asked if Teddy had had a tetanus shot, I said, 'No.' To my amazement, Teddy very clearly said, 'Yes.' And I remembered the whole team had had shots the day before we left London for this trip. Then he tried to squeeze my hand, couldn't, and started crying again. Somebody told me to check him into the hospital, and led the way to the admissions office while I kept yelling about X rays. When the girl asked me what religion Teddy was, I said, 'I don't think he's Jewish because we've been making jokes about that,' so I put him down as a Protestant. When I got back to EW [the Emergency Ward] they were getting ready to wheel him to the X-ray room. Just before he left I said, 'Don't worry, Teddy. You'll be all right.' But I walked out of there afraid he wouldn't make it through the night."

". . . I was watching the game with Dr. David Streater, the 67's physician," said Dr. Rudy Gittens, orthopedic resident at the Ottawa Civic Hospital. "As soon as Green was hit, we went right to the emergency room under the stands and were there when they brought him in. Considering his condition, he was astonishingly lucid. When both David and I noticed he had facial paralysis, I went over and said several times, 'Squeeze my fingers, John.' He just sat there, then suddenly exploded, 'Tell that SOB my name is Ted, not John.' I laughed, apologized, and asked him again to squeeze my fingers with both hands. His right was strong, but the left was weak. I thought at first he had a concussion, but when I touched the wound before putting in the stitch, I realized it was a depressed skull fracture. David agreed, and we ordered him to the hospital. David called Dr. Richard."

". . . At first I thought it was a simple laceration," said Dr. Streater, a chubby, blue-eyed, 31-year-old resident at the Ottawa General Hospital, who was with Dr. Gittens at the game. "But when I saw the drooping on the left side of the face and heard the slurring speech, I knew it was worse than that. After Rudy put in the stitch and felt the wound, I fingered it and agreed that it might be a compound depressed skull fracture. We get head injuries, mostly concussions, but very few fractures because Junior A hockey players are required to use helmets. I phoned Mike Richard and told him what we thought, and he said he'd go right to the hospital."

". . . I was a little surprised when Mr. Green asked for the last rites," said Fr. Jean-Paul Hupé, the hospital's gray-haired head chaplain, speaking in a heavy French accent. "Although I've given rites to people of all faiths, they're mostly Catholics. Mr. Green was entered as a Protestant, which I thought he was until he told me he was Catholic. Actually, he didn't get the last rites. That's what people used to call them, but now the last rites are given only after death. The sacrament we once called the last rites is really a prayer for the sick, and that's what I gave Mr. Green. From James 5:13:

"Is anyone among you suffering? Let him pray. Is anyone among you sick? Let him call the priests of the Church, and let them pray over him anointing him with oil in the name of the Lord; and the prayer of faith will save the sick man, and the Lord will raise him up; and if he has committed sins, he will be forgiven. Therefore, confess your sins to one another, and pray for one another, that you may be healed."

". . . My dad was taking the whole family out to celebrate my birthday, which was still a few days off, when David Streater called me," said Dr. Richard, an energetic young man who flies his own plane and is rapidly becoming one of the most sought-after neurosurgeons in Canada. "David told me Green had a serious injury, which he and Rudy Gittens agreed might be a compound depressed skull fracture. I arrived at the hospital at 8:50 P.M., a few minutes after Green was brought in. I recognized the seriousness of the injury, but not the extent. He was awake, quite lucid, knew where he was, and answered questions fairly quickly.

"I'm a hockey fan. I knew who he was, and I didn't like him until I got to know him because I root for the Canadiens. First thing I did was look at the patient and try to see what I was facing. You try to set the general injury. You see the cut in the parietal region of the right side of the head. The wound itself was nothing. You just put a small dressing on that. We had to look at the X rays to see if any bone was driven into the brain.

"While they were taking the films I phoned Ted's wife, Pat, who is a fine person. When I told her of the injury she took it well and didn't push any panic button. She was concerned and said she'd come right on. At the time I talked to her, I didn't know how bad it was. Sometimes it's obvious, but in Green's case it wasn't.

"When I looked at the pictures, we got him right up to the operating room. They showed both the depression—bone driven into the brain—and the obvious compound, which simply means the skin is broken. In the operating room I shaved Green myself. They call me 'The Barber' because I do the shaving in 90 percent of my surgery. We had a little byplay about the shave. I told him I was going to take those nice curls off and asked if he wanted a bean shave or an Iroquois cut. Of course I really wasn't making light of it, but I didn't want him too upset. I knew he had requested and received the last rites of the Catholic Church, but he was in no danger of dying. He may have thought he was going to die, but I didn't.

"After I shaved his head, he was put to sleep," Dr. Richard went on. "We opened the laceration. In EW he had paralysis of one side of his face, some weakness in his left hand, and some speech difficulty. This guy is left-handed and his speech center is on the right side. He happened to be hit in a perfect spot to do the most damage—right in the area that controls the speech and left arm and leg. I couldn't tell whether his weakness and paralysis were progressive, because they were no worse in the operating room than they had been an hour before when he came into the hospital. But I think all his trouble was related to the actual bone fragments that had been driven in.

"What you do is extend the laceration and use it as one limb of the skull opening. The bone is underneath, and you can get at it. He had bone fragments. In other words, it was comminuted—more than one fragment—with lacerations [tearing] of the dura, which is the covering of the brain. He also had a cut into his brain. There was one very large fragment of bone, which was lifted off fairly freely, and other small fragments were removed. It was when we saw those fragments and lacerations of the brain and of the dura that we realized the injury was more serious than we anticipated.

"The operation took about 2½ hours. He had a fairly significant amount of bruising of the scalp and muscles in the area because it was a blunt, low-velocity injury. When you have a blunt injury you get a lot of bruising, not like a gunshot wound, where all you have is a small hole for an injury. In a case like Green's, what you do after all the bone fragments are removed is close the cover of the brain and put the scalp flap back in, leaving the hole there for the present. You then cover it in a later operation with plastic or steel. I was pleased. I felt things had gone very well. Just as I finished, Pat called. I had promised to call her when the operation was over, but she phoned first. I told her what we had done and she said she'd be flying in from Winnipeg the next day."

". . . In the locker room between periods of the game,

all any of us talked about was Teddy," said Eddie Westfall. "They had taken him to the hospital and the reports we got were skimpy and unreliable. There was even a rumor he had died. On the ice, on the bench, everywhere I went that night I couldn't think about anything but Teddy. We broke into the Bruins together and were teammates and close friends for eight years. The only reason we don't see much of each other now is that we live so far apart—he's in Lynnfield and I have a place up in Pelham, New Hampshire.

"By the time the game ended, we finally did get an accurate report—that Teddy had a skull fracture—but we didn't know how bad it was. I dressed fast, got into a cab alone, and told the driver to take me to the Ottawa General Hospital. There was an intern on the desk who was a hockey fan and recognized my name when I told him who I was.

" 'I'm concerned about Teddy,' I said. 'What's the latest on him?'

" 'He's still in the operating room,' the guy answered. 'It looks like he'll be in there for some time yet.'

" 'Can you tell me anything about his condition?'

" 'His skull is fractured and there may be other complications. They have to relieve the pressure on his brain.'

" 'I want to wait around,' I said.

"It was about eleven-thirty or twelve, and he said, 'It may be a long time.'

"'If it doesn't matter to you,' I said, 'I'd just as soon wait.'

"'Why don't you do this?' he suggested. 'There's a recreation room at the interns' quarters across the street. Go on in there, watch TV or something, and as soon as I have any news I'll get it to you.'

"I thanked him and went over to what appeared to be a dorm, and joined some guys watching a movie on TV. During the commercials I told them who I was and asked them about Teddy, but they didn't have anything to tell me. A little after one o'clock, the intern I had originally talked to came over and said, 'He's out of the operating room. Everything has gone well and Dr. Richard is very pleased. He's with Teddy in the recovery room, but he'll be leaving there pretty soon.'

"'When can I see Teddy?'

"'I don't know if you can. Dr. Richard is very tough about stuff like that.'

"'I don't care,' I said. 'I want to see Teddy so I can go back and tell the guys how he's doing.'

"'I know what you mean. I'll see what I can do.'

"I was in summer clothes and happened to be wearing white shoes. This intern got me a white doctor's smock and white trousers and a white face mask and said, 'Follow me.' We went back into the hospital and up the elevator to the sixth floor. As we got off we ran into a doctor in a green operating outfit and a couple of nurses. Down the hall, I could hear other nurses yelling, 'Mr. Green, Mr.

Green,' and making slapping noises. The guy was Dr. Richard, and he was annoyed as hell to see me there. The intern with me said, 'This is Eddie Westfall of the Bruins. He wants to see Teddy.'

" 'Well, he has no business up here,' Dr. Richard said.

" 'I know it doesn't mean anything to you, Doctor,' I said, 'but hockey players are a closely knit group and we want to know what's happening to Teddy. All I want to do is look at him.'

" 'You're not going into the recovery room.'

" 'I'm going in whether you want me to or not,' I said. 'If I just walk to the door and look in I'll be satisfied. I don't think you're going to stop me.' I walked away and down to the room where the nurses were calling Teddy's name. Teddy was on a stretcher-type bed, moaning, the only patient in a big room with other beds. The two nurses kept yelling at him and jostling him pretty good. I was surprised they cuffed him around so soon after the operation, but I figured they must have known what they were doing. I went in, stood by the side of the bed, and asked the nurses why they were calling his name and belting him. One said, 'We're trying to wake him up.'

" 'Have you been ordered to do this?'

" 'In a case like this, they want the patient awake as soon as possible. We have to do it fast so we can get responses to certain tests—feel the ends of his fingers and other parts of his left side to see what he can do,' she replied.

"I watched them slap and yell for about 15 minutes, getting nothing but moans and no movement, so I said, 'Mind if I try?'

" 'If you think you can wake him up, go ahead,' one said.

"I took his hand. 'Greenie, it's 18.' Instead of calling me Ed, the guys call me by my uniform number. Teddy didn't move, and I said, 'It's 18. Can you hear me? If you can, squeeze my hand.' He squeezed my hand, and I felt like a new father who just got the news that mother and infant are doing fine.

" 'It's 18,' I said. 'If you can hear me, say something." Teddy stirred and mumbled.

" 'You know who it is, Greenie?'

"He said something that sounded like 'Yes.'

" 'Do you feel any pain?'

" 'No,' he said, quite distinctly.

" 'Can you hear me?'

"That 'yes' sound again. The nurses began telling me what to do and what to ask him. I must have been in there an hour altogether before they thanked me and said they could now handle it. The last thing I did was ask if it meant anything bad that Teddy never opened his eyes, and they said it didn't. Then I went downstairs, changed into my regular clothes, thanked the intern and apologized to him—Dr. Richard must have given him hell—and took a cab to the hotel. It was almost three in the morning, but the boys were all up, and I told them everything I could."

". . . I guess it was around eight-thirty—in Winnipeg

we're an hour behind Ottawa—when I first got the call," Pat said. "When the man told me he was Dr. Michael Richard, I thought for a minute it was some kind of a gag, because it sounded like 'Maurice' and I wondered why Maurice Richard, who still lived in Montreal, would be posing as a doctor from Ottawa. Then I realized this was another Richard, and he was telling me Teddy had a depressed skull fracture and was going into surgery. I had no idea what a depressed skull fracture was, but I felt a little better when the doctor told me he was sure Teddy would be all right. I told him I'd try to get to Ottawa the next day, and he said he'd call when the operation was over. When I asked how long it would take, he said anywhere from an hour and a half on, depending on the circumstances. Of course, I was frightened to death, but I had to stay calm because of Teddy's mother. She's very nervous and I knew it would upset her if I told her right out of the blue. She always listens to the 11 P.M. news while waiting for Teddy's dad to get home from work, and I was sure they'd have his injury on it. I didn't want his mother to be alone then, so I called his father at work and he said he'd get home before eleven.

"Then Milt Schmidt phoned. He didn't have anything new to tell me except that I shouldn't worry about expenses—the Bruins would take care of everything, including transportation from Winnipeg to Ottawa if I decided to come. He also said he'd arrange for me to stay at the Chateau Laurier, which is within walking distance of the hospital. Then Eddie Johnston, Teddy's best friend on the club, called to say he'd meet me if I went.

"I waited and waited for Dr. Richard to call, and when he hadn't by midnight, which was 1 A.M. in Ottawa, I couldn't stand it any longer and called him. First I got the intern who assisted him in the operation, then Dr. Richard himself came on to say he was just about to call me. He explained the whole operation and said he was quite pleased. He said there would be some paralysis, but told me not to worry about it because he was sure it would be only temporary. I told him I would be in the next day, and he said that was fine and he'd be glad to talk to me when I arrived. I felt better, made a few calls to the family, and then went to bed."

Chapter / 3

My first memory after the operation was waking up to see Phil Esposito, Bobby Orr, and Eddie Johnston at my bedside. There wasn't much conversation—at least on my part—because, while conscious and aware of my surroundings, I could hardly express myself at all. Everything I said was so garbled that my speech control seemed almost nonexistent.

Johnston, my closest friend on the club, did most of the talking, kidding me about not being badly hurt because I had been hit on the head. I don't recall either Espi or Bobby saying anything except maybe to tell me everything was going to be OK. But I guess all three were pretty shook up when they saw me with my head bandaged, my speech a mess, and my left hand paralyzed. I'm told that later in the morning Milt Schmidt came up, but I don't remember seeing him.

I have no memory of Eddie Westfall's part in my coming around right after the operation. Doctors and nurses told me about that. Some didn't even know who he was—only a big guy who wouldn't take "no" for an answer and insisted on seeing me.

Actually, although I'd now undergone the operation, that first day was much the same as the hour immediately after Maki hit me. Instead of memories, I have a jumble of impressions, including Pat's arrival and her kissing me hello. I didn't know when she got there, or how, or who she was with, or who brought her to the hospital. I didn't know where she was staying or how long she planned to remain.

One thing I do remember is Dr. Richard coming in, talking a few minutes, feeling my left side, and telling me I was doing well and might be able to go home the following Sunday. I think Pat was there at the time, but I'm not sure. The news I had a chance to leave so soon was a pleasant surprise. During a lucid moment now and then, I had convinced myself I'd probably be in the hospital for weeks.

At one point that first day after the operation, I tried to remember how I had been hurt and by whom. My last memory was of Wayne Maki down in front of me on the ice. Although I didn't remember anybody telling me (practically everyone who talked to me did, and I myself had wanted to get him for hitting me), I decided as I lay on the hospital bed that Maki must have been the one who hit me. I couldn't remember anybody else on the St. Louis team being nearby, so it had to be Maki. However, I didn't really know for sure until I was told that day—I think by Eddie Johnston, who came back to see me in the afternoon.

I kept blacking out, or perhaps dropping off to sleep, whether anyone was in the room with me or not. I remember being terribly tired all the time. I didn't realize it then, but later I learned that I was awakened every half hour around the clock for vital signs, and made several trips out of the room for encephalograph readings (EEG's). But I felt no pain—just a dull haziness like the night before, right after I was hurt.

". . . Early the next morning after Teddy got hurt," Pat said, "his parents and his brother and sister-in-law, Tony and Mary, came over. By then I already had a reservation on an 11 A.M. flight to Ottawa, and was waiting for a phone call from Eddie Johnston, who said he would meet me at the airport. Teddy's folks were taking Karen with them, and were going to deliver the boys, Chris and Brian, to my mother. While we were sitting around, Tony said, 'Gee, Pat, I hate to see you go alone. Why don't I get a few days off and go with you?'

"'You don't have to do that, Tony,' I said. 'Wait until I get there. Then if I feel somebody should be with me, I'll phone.'

" 'I'll go with you,' Mary said. 'It's easier for me than Tony to get time off.'

"Mary works for an insurance company and Tony is on the police force. I really didn't want to go to Ottawa alone, so it took very little persuading for me to agree to have Mary come along. Right after I phoned the airline to make her reservation, Eddie called from Ottawa and I told him what plane we'd be on and when we'd arrive.

"We got a paper at the Winnipeg airport, and there were pictures on the front page of the fight between Teddy and Maki. The last one in the sequence, which showed Teddy on the ice with that terrible blank look on his face, scared me to death. As soon as we were settled aboard the airplane, I started talking about Teddy, wondering how bad he was, and if he'd ever come out of it or ever be right again. Mary kept trying to get me to change the subject, but I couldn't. All I could think of was that picture of Teddy.

"I don't remember either of us saying anything about the possibility of his dying, but every time that picture flashed through my mind, I wondered. I knew I wouldn't really get the situation straight until I talked to the doctor, but it was hard to believe anything good. The best I could expect was that Teddy would have some sort of permanent disability. I mentioned that to Mary, and she kept assuring me he would be all right. Of course, she didn't know any more about it than I did, but it was comforting because she said what I wanted to hear.

"Eddie Johnston was at the airport when we arrived in Ottawa about one-thirty in the afternoon. As soon as we got our luggage, he said, 'Do you want to check in at the hotel first or go right to the hospital?'
" 'The hospital.'
" 'OK.'
" 'How's Teddy?'
" 'He's coming along.'
" 'Meaning?'
" 'Well,' Eddie replied, 'his speech is a little funny. Otherwise, he's all right.'
" 'Come on, Eddie,' I said. 'Tell me the truth. How bad is he?'
" 'He's going to be all right, Pat.'
" 'How much paralysis?'
" 'Oh—uh—he's having a little trouble with his left hand, but the doctor says it will be all right.'
" 'His leg?'
" 'No problem,' Eddie said. 'His leg's fine.'
"All the way to the hospital, I kept asking about Teddy, and Eddie kept trying to change the subject. As soon as we arrived, I rushed up to Teddy's room, stopped at the door, peered in, and thought, *My God, he looks terrible.* His eyes were closed, the left side of his face was lopsided, and he had a huge bandage wound around his head like a turban. I hesitated long enough to compose myself, then went into the room, walked over to the bed, and bent down and kissed him.

"He opened his eyes, tried to smile, and mumbled, 'What are you doing here?' Then he closed his eyes again. His voice shocked me, it was so bad. Because of needing to be awakened every half hour, he was obviously exhausted, so after greeting him I left the room to talk to his nurse. She couldn't tell me much, but said Dr. Richard would be around later. Then Eddie took Mary and me to the Chateau Laurier and checked us in.

"When I met Dr. Richard at the hospital later, I was amazed how young he was," Pat went on. "He didn't seem much older than Teddy. Though busy, he was affable and friendly. He told me Teddy was doing all right, and promised to talk longer to me later in the week, which he did. We sat down in the hospital lounge one day and he gave me a thorough briefing on the operation and Teddy's progress, which he told me was very good. I then said, 'Please, Doctor, level with me. Is Teddy's condition all that good?'

" 'So far,' he said. 'But in these cases, there's always a chance of convulsions which might cause a setback.'

" 'I wish I hadn't asked,' I said.

" 'Well, don't worry, Mrs. Green. We haven't seen any signs of trouble. It's just that we want to be ready if it comes.'

"All of which shook me up no end, but there was one more question I had to ask: Would there be any aftereffects? The doctor's reply was a little vague, but understandably so. He told me it was hard to say at this point, but if there were no complications, Teddy might quite possibly come out of this without any serious physical handicaps. That made me feel a little better."

". . . When I went with Bobby and Phil to see Teddy at the hospital the morning after he was hurt," said Eddie Johnston, "I did most of the talking because the other guys were so affected. Bobby said something, then had to turn away because he was crying. All Phil could say was, 'You look fine, Teddy.' Of course, he didn't—he looked terrible—but I kidded him by saying, 'How could you have an operation on your head? There's nothing in it.' Although he doesn't remember, he grinned and mumbled something.

"As soon as I found out when Pat would arrive, I got permission from Milt Schmidt to stay in Ottawa for a couple of days. I missed an exhibition game with Toronto the night after Teddy was hurt, and didn't rejoin the team until Tuesday.

"Pat was great, composed and appreciative when I met her and her sister-in-law at the airport. The only way she showed her concern was by drilling me about Teddy all the way to the hospital.

"By the time I left Tuesday, Teddy was somewhat better, and Pat told me whenever I phoned during the week that he was steadily improving."

I felt much better on Tuesday, the second day following the operation—more alert and more aware of people around me, especially Pat and Eddie. But the constant fatigue never left, because the nurses continued to wake me regularly. As I look back now, this seems one of the worst problems for anyone who has brain surgery. The danger of a sudden change in condition is so constant that medical people don't dare let a patient go very long without the kind of tests he can take only when awake.

Pat and Eddie continued to be deeply concerned, although they kept joking about my bald head and my having to wear a wig until my hair grew back. However, neither fooled me, because I caught them exchanging occasional glances. I guess I still looked like hell. The left side of my face was pulled down, which caused my speech impairment, and I couldn't move my left hand.

It bothered me when Dr. Richard took the bandages off my head to examine the wound and the tubes he had put in for a drain. There was fluid, and more came when he squeezed my head—enough to saturate my pillow. But the doctor told me it was nothing to worry about, and again said he thought I'd be able to go home the following Sunday.

I improved steadily during the rest of the week. From the first day, I got up to go to the bathroom, leaning on a nurse or whoever was around. I don't remember doing this on Monday or Tuesday, but from Wednesday through Friday my memory is pretty sharp.

By Wednesday I was sitting up, and a nurse asked me if I wanted her to shave me.

"Hell, no," I said. "I can shave myself."

I'd forgotten my left hand was still paralyzed, and that I had to shave with my right. I cut myself a few times, but I got the job done. I didn't want anyone to do anything for me, figuring the more I did myself, the faster I'd get better. I didn't want to be catered to or babied. Even though it was exhausting to walk around the bed or take the few steps to the bathroom, it always felt good to be on my feet, but the fact that I tired so easily bothered the hell out of me.

So did recollections of my stupidity on the ice, which really got to me those first few days in the hospital. I kept thinking back to the fight and blaming myself for what happened. This was the first time I had ever been hit in a hockey hassle and not seen the blow coming. I didn't blame Maki—after all, he was a rookie trying to make the NHL, which he had failed to do his first time around. And even though he undoubtedly lost his head, I'm sure he felt winning a one-on-one fight with me would be a big plus for him, and that I, Terrible Teddy Green, should have had sense enough to watch him until he skated away. This must have been the biggest thing on my mind, because I talked a lot about it. Pat and everyone else tried to tell me it was over and done with and I should forget it. But I couldn't.

Over Pat's objections, I insisted on calling my mother in Winnipeg the fourth day after the operation—on Thursday. By then, they were letting me walk out of the room to the nurses' station, which was only a few steps away. I knew my speech was bad, but I felt good otherwise. Pat thought my calling would upset both Mother and me. Before the injury, I never showed much emotion about anything. Even when I spent the better part of two seasons in and out of hospitals with knee problems, I had never given way to my feelings. But now I was emotional about everything—seeing Pat and the guys from the team, watching letters and telegrams of encouragement pile up so fast that it would take months to acknowledge them all, accepting the wonderful help from the nurses (especially a jolly, middle-aged one we all called Mama Schwartz), even talking to Dr. Richard. I don't remember when I had last cried, but now I seemed to cry over something every day. Pat, well aware of this, didn't want me to do anything that would set me off again, like a phone call home. Besides, since she knows my mother as well as I do, she was sure that, rather than reassure her, a call from me would simply make her feel worse because of my speech.

I phoned home in the morning, before Pat arrived at the hospital, and the minute the call went through, I realized she had been right. To begin with, Karen, my daughter, who was then five, answered the phone, and just hearing her talk shook me up. As I listened, tears began rolling down my cheeks, making my speech even worse. And when I said a badly garbled, "Hello, honey," she said, "Daddy, why does your voice sound so funny?"

When my mother got on, I tried to talk as if there

wasn't anything wrong. But you can't make a fuzzy voice sound natural, and I hadn't said three words before I heard Mom stifle a sob. Then my Uncle Bob (Dad's brother, who had just dropped by) took the phone and asked how I was.

"Fine," I said.

"Are you sure?"

"Positive."

Then he said, "Hold on a second. Your mother can talk now."

These few words with Bob helped me pull myself together, but that didn't last long because Mom was sobbing, which set me off and made talking even harder for me. She finally managed to say, "You shouldn't have called, Ted, but I'm glad you did. At least I know you can use the phone."

After we had said good-bye, I realized my speech was much worse than I thought and calling home had been a mistake. I was shaking and crying from emotional strain, and upset at myself for having put Mother through such an ordeal. All I had accomplished was to disturb us both and make things tougher for the nurses because they had to settle me. Later, I broke down telling Pat about the call, and she had to calm me all over again.

Despite my condition, we had a few laughs that first week in the hospital. One, which Pat didn't think at all funny although it tickled me, was a note from Larry Mann, a friend who's a character actor in Los Angeles.

All it consisted of was a newspaper clipping headlined "Green Has 2½-Hour Brain Operation." Underneath Mann had scribbled, "Dear Ted—Sorry to hear about your accident, but I know it can't be serious because I've known you long enough to know that you haven't got a goddam brain in your head."

When I showed the clipping to Mike Richard (we were on a first-name basis from the beginning), he laughed and said, "You think that's funny? When I got inside your head, all I saw were two cells, and they weren't even connected."

I had no formal therapy during the week, probably because nobody thought I needed it. The paralysis on the left side had never affected my leg or any part of my arm from the shoulder to the wrist. My speech improved daily. Feeling began to return in my left hand the second day after the operation, so I soon could move it fairly well. The only real trouble seemed to be with the fingers of my left hand, which were inert at first. The nurses made me exercise them by trying to squeeze a little gadget they gave me. This developed feeling in all but the thumb, which remained stiff and immovable. That didn't bother me too much in spite of what the doctor said. Although he encouraged me about almost full recovery, he told me he had strong doubts the thumb would ever come back. At that point, the uppermost thought in my mind was how I could handle a hockey stick with a numb thumb. Anyhow, who needs a thumb to play hockey? By Friday I was really chipper, not just about my rapid improvement but because Mike was so certain I could go home Sunday—barring unforeseen complications—that he told Pat she could reserve our plane tickets.

After Eddie Johnston went back to London, Ontario, to rejoin the Bruins, he phoned Pat daily to see how I was doing. Friday they let me talk with him, and I got so excited that my speech, confused enough to start with, became practically unintelligible. Eddie pulled me out of it very quickly by saying, "Hey, Dum-Dum, how the hell do you expect me to understand you when you talk like that?" And from then on Johnston called me "Dum-Dum" whenever we talked.

("When I talked to him that day and started the 'Dum-Dum' business," Johnston said, "his speech wasn't really so bad—much better than when I had seen him. Maybe ribbing him about a thing that serious sounds cruel, as making fun of anybody with a physical handicap always is, but hockey players get hurt so often that this is really our only way of handling a situation like Teddy's. Maybe it's our way of softening the blow. Or of making the injured guy feel better. Or of keeping our own sanity.")

Friday night or early Saturday morning—I had no idea exactly when—I woke up doing one hell of a dance in bed. My whole body was shaking as if I were a monkey on a string, and my head hurt something awful. When I put my hand up to the right side of my head, it seemed swollen, and I quickly checked it by touching the left side, which was smaller and apparently normal. I didn't know what was happening, except that it couldn't be good and I needed help. I pushed the nurse's button, but the one on duty must have been making rounds or something. Nobody came for what seemed like ages. I kept pressing and pressing, and finally the supervising nurse walked in, took one look at my swollen head and quivering body, and, without a word, turned around and left. I could hear her running. She then came back and told me she was trying to get hold of Dr. Shirama. I distinctly remember telling her to phone Dr. Richard at his home in Hull, Quebec, just across the Ottawa River and about 20 minutes from the hospital. She told me she would, and ran back to her station to call him.

While I continued to quiver and the right side of my head felt as if it were about to explode, the nurse kept coming in and going out. I have no recollection of time at all, but I remember her telling me she had reached Dr. Richard and that he would arrive any minute. She had also located Dr. Shirama, who was on his way to my room. The two doctors met at the door, but talked only briefly because Mike came right over, saw my shaking body and the swelling, and immediately ordered me upstairs to the operating room on the sixth floor.

The last thing I remember was that horrible sickly feeling of anesthesia going into my lungs, and saying to Mike Richard, as he stood over me in his green smock, "I'm sorry I had to get you out of bed in the middle of the night." I don't know if he heard me or not, because at that point I passed out.

"... When the doctor told me Friday he thought Teddy could go home Sunday, I felt marvelous," Pat said. "I figured he really was out of the woods. Except for his thumb, practically all the paralysis was gone. Of course, there was the business of having to return to Ottawa to get a plate put into his head, but the doctor made pretty light of that. He said that would not be for a few months, and the operation wasn't too bad. So Friday night I went back to the Chateau feeling happy, confident everything was fine.

"Just as I was preparing to leave for the hospital at about nine Saturday morning, Dr. Richard phoned the hotel.

" 'We had to take Teddy up for surgery during the night,' he said.

" 'My God, why didn't you call me?'

" 'It was about three-thirty in the morning. There was no point in robbing you of a night's sleep. You couldn't have done anything anyhow.'

" 'Well, I'm coming down right now.'

" 'Why don't you wait half an hour or so?' he said gently. 'He's in the recovery room.'

" 'What happened? Is he all right?'

"'He's going to be. I'll explain when you get here.'

"I fiddled around the room a while, then walked through Parliament Park to the hospital. When I got there, they told me Teddy was still in the recovery room on the sixth floor, but Dr. Richard had left permission for me to go up. I was shocked at what I saw. Teddy was jerking and bouncing around on a table, his head freshly bandaged, with tubes sticking out. A nurse was watching him closely while she rubbed his back with some sort of ointment. But the most discouraging thing was to see Dr. Richard sitting on a bed with his head in his hands and looking terribly dejected.

" 'Is he in convulsions?' I said.

"Dr. Richard looked up, his eyes red from too little sleep and too much work. He smiled slightly. 'I didn't expect you so soon.'

" 'I hurried.'

"He nodded toward the table Teddy was on and said, 'He's reacting to the anesthetic.'

"I didn't know whether the doctor was telling the truth or not, and I didn't dare ask. But I did want to know what happened.

" 'He hemorrhaged and went into convulsions,' the doctor said. 'There was pressure on the brain and we had to get rid of it quickly.'

"I put my hand over my mouth and took a deep breath to keep from crying out, then managed to ask how bad it was.

" 'We don't know yet. We can't get any movement out of his left arm or his left leg.'

" 'You mean his whole side is paralyzed?'

"The doctor nodded but told me not to panic—that he'd seen people in the same condition come back practically all the way.

"I stayed in the room about three hours. I didn't want to leave Teddy because I was afraid he would die—a question I hadn't dared ask the doctor, who was in and out all morning. Finally, around one o'clock in the afternoon, when Teddy still hadn't come out of the anesthetic, I knew I had to call home. The family was expecting us the next day, but of course there was now no chance of our leaving.

" 'What shall I tell his mom and dad?' I asked.

" 'Whatever you think best.'

" 'Is it serious enough for them to come here?'

"Dr. Richard didn't come right out and say Ted might die, but I felt he considered it a possibility when he said, 'I'll leave that up to you. He's a pretty sick boy. If you feel his parents should be here, by all means tell them to come.'

"So I phoned Ted's parents, told them as much as I knew, and before I had a chance to ask them, they said they'd come. They called back later to tell me what plane they'd be on, and we arranged to meet at the Chateau, where I'd reserved a room for them. While I tried to appear calm, I was so distraught I can't remember whether I ate or what else I did. All I could think of was my husband: Would he live, and, if so, would he ever be normal?

I never thought about his chances of playing hockey again."

". . . The morning after Teddy got hurt," said Esposito, "he looked so bad I don't think any of us knew what to expect. For all we knew, we'd never see him alive again. I've seen some pretty bad injuries and had a few myself, but nothing like this.

"He improved during the week," Esposito went on. "Everything looked great until he had that hemorrhage. When we heard how much worse off it left him, I went to Father Wright, the Catholic priest in London, Ontario, and asked if he would have a Mass for Teddy. He said he'd be happy to if I served. I didn't know too much about it. I had to read stuff I hadn't read for years—ever since I was a kid. Every single person in training camp, Catholic and otherwise, was there. We got a get-well Mass card, which we all signed and sent to Teddy. The priest was very nice. He understood our feelings and shared them with us."

". . . I waited until after the hemorrhage crisis was over before telling Teddy about the Mass," Pat said. "It was such a moving thing that he openly wept. Next to his family, the team players are closest to Teddy, and the special Mass meant so much to him that he was completely overcome."

". . . The hospital called me at about three o'clock Saturday morning," said Dr. Richard. "Ted had experienced a sudden headache, there was swelling, and his left side was paralyzing. I had seen him that afternoon and he seemed OK. It was obvious what had happened. There was no question in my mind that he was hemorrhaging and getting new pressure on the brain. It's not normal or frequent, but it's a possibility you always watch for in a case of this type.

"What happens is you have scalp laceration. The problem is the scalp has been closed, and usually the brain and its covering are protected by bone. But the bone had been removed in surgery, and this bone defect had not yet been repaired. Therefore if you bleed underneath the scalp, there's no protection for the brain and nowhere for the blood to go but there.

"This was a sudden delayed hemorrhage," Dr. Richard went on. "Scalp swollen right side. Completely paralyzed left side. I don't remember if he had any fine movements [ability to feel anything with his fingertips] at all. We sent him right up to the operating room. This thing had to be opened immediately and rapidly. He was concerned because of the speed with which we took him into surgery. He knew by that alone it was an emergency situation.

"I thought the bleeding was from one of the blood vessels that run between the bone and the scalp—they supply blood to the scalp. I wasn't sure, but I thought this was related to the bruising from the original injury. I had to reopen the scalp and drain the blood off the brain, making sure it was all out before closing the scalp again. You hate to touch that area any more than you have to, because when you do you know it's going to cause some paralysis. Before that hemorrhage, almost all Teddy's original paralysis had disappeared. His face was still a little affected, but it was coming back and his speech was improving. After the hemorrhage, his whole left side was paralyzed. If he hadn't hemorrhaged, he would have been out of the hospital a day or so later and I don't think he would have had any paralysis at all.

"Following the hemorrhage, I didn't think he would ever play hockey again, although I didn't tell him that. Maybe I mentioned it to him later—I don't recall. But now he had definite paralysis that appeared much more likely to be permanent than it had before."

I don't remember being too shook about Dr. Richard coming in and getting me up to the operating room so fast—in fact, as soon as he arrived I felt safer and more confident that, with him to look after me, everything would be all right. I knew I was in trouble, although I had no idea how serious it was. The next few days all run together in my mind. I didn't know what was happening, and I was too sick to care. It was just as well. If I had been aware of developments over the next 72 hours, I'd probably have thrown in the towel.

Chapter / 4

My impressions of those days following the second operation are a mad jumble of confused, unrelated memories, much like the hours after I got hurt. I remember my throat being very sore. I remember Dr. Richard bending over me while I wondered why he was trying to choke me. I remember Pat coming in and out of the room from time to time. I remember being terribly sick to my stomach. I remember seeing my mother and father, and I remember Dad staying in the room a long, long time. I remember not being able to feel anything on my left side. I remember a strange doctor working over me and talking to me. I remember my leg dragging when I walked, but I don't remember getting in and out of bed. I remember asking the doctor if my leg would get better, and I remember him telling me it *was* getting better. I remember asking him not to hide anything from me, and I remember him saying he didn't think my arm would ever come back.

I remember a long succession of people coming in and out of my room, but don't remember how I got there from the recovery room. I remember seeing unfamiliar-looking machines being brought in. I remember crying a good deal. I remember thinking about my brothers, and once I dreamed about going hunting with them. I thought about playing golf with them or with friends, and I remember hoping I could play again because I loved it. I remember the strange doctor standing in the doorway shrugging his shoulders, as if he wasn't sure what to do. I remember Pat putting a handkerchief to her eyes, and I remember wondering why because I hadn't seen her cry.

And I remember thinking I was going to die. Or maybe hoping I would because I thought I might be a vegetable —a lifetime burden on Pat and the rest of the family.

I don't remember any thoughts of hockey, although sometimes flashes of my closest Bruin friends—Eddie Johnston and Bobby Orr particularly—crossed my mind. Nor do I remember wishing I could play hockey again, probably because all hope of doing that seemed gone. With my career apparently over, I guess I had a mental blackout regarding it.

My first really sharp memories date from the third or fourth day after the hemorrhage. The first thing I noticed was that my legs seemed tightly wedged together. It turned out that sandbags were propped against them to keep them straight. The sandbags were removable so I could get in and out of bed. My left foot still dragged a little, but it had already come back most of the way. My left arm was paralyzed, and, with the left side of my face still pulled down, my speech was worse than right after the injury. In fact, the hemorrhage had done more damage than Wayne Maki's stick.

Confused impressions were all I had of those days after the second operation. Only from others could I learn what really went on during that period.

"... I had to go to Detroit," Dr. Richard said, "but I waited until the last minute to leave, on account of Ted. Pat reached the hospital much faster than I expected her to, and Ted hadn't come completely out of the anesthetic when she got there. I had put pressure on his throat until he showed signs of waking up, then turned him over to a nurse to keep him rubbed down and watch his movements. Dead tired, I sat on one of the beds with my head in my hands. I think Pat thought I was discouraged, but I wasn't. The operation had gone well, and there were no signs of further complications, but of course it was too early to tell what might happen.

"In my absence, Dr. L. P. Ivan, the chief of neurosurgery at the hospital, was going to cover for me. Although we work independently, we cover for each other when one of us goes away. I was concerned about Ted, but I knew he would be in good hands. Dr. Ivan is an excellent neurosurgeon, and could handle any emergencies that came up."

"... I didn't know Mr. Green until I took over his case,"

said Dr. Ivan, a middle-aged Hungarian who speaks with a slight but unmistakable accent. "I'm not a hockey fan and have never seen a game in my life, so his name meant nothing to me except as a patient. Dr. Richard briefed me before he left, and I knew how Mr. Green got hurt and the medical history of what followed.

"Never having met a professional hockey player, I expected a rough, somewhat obnoxious individual, but in Mr. Green I found a calm, pleasant person and a polite, considerate, thoroughly cooperative patient. He often apologized for putting me out, and was really a joy to work with. He doesn't remember much about being under my care, because throughout that time he was a very sick young man whose condition deteriorated in the first few days after his second operation.

"As sometimes happens in cases like Mr. Green's, new pressures on the brain were building up, and for a couple of days I seriously considered more surgery. However, I was most anxious to avoid it, if possible, because every time you go into the brain you damage more cells. Furthermore, I hesitated to operate so soon after he had already undergone surgery. He was suffering serious paralysis. He couldn't move his left arm, the left side of his face was paralyzed, and his left leg was affected, although that appeared to be coming along well.

"It was about the only thing that was getting better. In all other aspects, Mr. Green gave every indication of undergoing continued brain pressure. He was drowsy, the weakness of his arm and face was very marked, and the right side of his head remained swollen. I had a suspicion that he might still be bleeding, in which case I would have to go in again to save his life.

"He could carry on a conversation," Dr. Ivan went on. "He didn't remember any of it later, but this is normal in such a case. His speech was bad, but you could understand him. He seemed to be in some pain, although that didn't appear to worry him as much as the prognosis for the future. When he asked me not to hide anything from him, I told him that, in my opinion, his left arm would always be paralyzed. It apparently was one of the few things he did remember.

"The drowsiness and motor weakness and head swelling continued through Tuesday. We had already had some difficult days trying to decide whether or not to operate, and time was not necessarily on our side. We had started giving him drugs—cortisone, hypertonic solutions, and mannitol, a concentrated drug administered into a vein—to counteract the brain swelling and save some of those nerve cells. If he hadn't had surgery so recently, I would have operated by then, but I was still hoping the medication would work.

"I kept his family as well informed as I could. His wife, a fine, beautiful, sensitive young woman, handled herself marvelously well. I talked to her mostly, although once when we thought we might have to operate, I told Mr. Green's father. I think the patient's wife, who had been under awful pressures right along, just couldn't face any more, and she asked Mr. Green, Senior, to find out what was going on. The worst days were Monday and Tuesday, and I had to be prepared to operate on very short notice.

"The younger Mrs. Green was afraid for his life, but I had no thought that he might die, and told her so. However, I did wonder how well he would function, which was why I kept putting off surgery. If we could pull him out of trouble without it, there was much less chance of a more extended permanent disability. Even without surgery, I didn't think his arm would come back. With it, there would be more brain damage and the eventual effect would have been impossible to predict.

"Finally—I think it was Wednesday morning—he suddenly started to improve. His head swelling began subsiding. The drowsiness was still there, but not as marked. His face looked better and his speech was clearer. By Wednesday afternoon I was sure he would be all right without surgery. But until then, it was touch and go."

". . . We didn't arrive in Ottawa until nearly midnight Saturday," said Jack Green, Ted's father, who works in the investigation department of the Canadian National Railroad in Winnipeg. "Pat tried to act calm when we met her at the hotel, but I could see she wasn't. Of course, she had been under some strain during the week and heavy pressure all day. She had also experienced a terrible disappointment, because she awoke that morning thinking she could take Ted home in pretty good shape the next day.

Now she knew he wouldn't be out of the hospital for weeks, and she had no idea how he'd be when he left.

"The three of us—my wife, Pat, and I—went to the hospital the next morning, and I didn't think Ted looked too bad. His face was twisted and he slurred his words, but we could understand him and he seemed to understand us. That night the two women went back to the hotel, but I stayed with Ted. He had special nurses, and two came in to check him every half hour. But it just isn't the same as having someone close to you at your bedside all night. Although Ted kept mumbling, "Oh, for crissakes, why don't you go to bed?" I think he was glad I stayed. I told him to forget it—I'm used to working nights and it was easy for me to stay awake.

"I sat at his bedside, wetting his lips and wiping his brow and just watching him. When he wanted to go to the bathroom, I helped him out of bed and put his good arm—the right—around my neck so he could lean on me. We walked very slowly because he was so weak, and his left foot dragged. I'm sure he would have been better off using a bedpan, but he flatly refused. No matter how sick he was—and he got sicker while we were there—he insisted on getting up to go to the bathroom.

"After getting him back into bed, I stretched him out and he tried to move his leg. Once, he told me to look under the blanket because he thought he was moving it, and sure enough, he was pushing with his foot. The nurse told him it was fine and he should keep working on it, and he did. I don't think he remembered my being there all night, although he did say he knew I was around for a long time.

"Pat, who was wonderfully composed and always optimistic, finally cracked Monday or Tuesday. She just fell apart from a whole combination of things—the pressures of the original injury, the events of the week before we were there, and then the much worse effects of Ted's hemorrhage. She broke down in the hallway outside Ted's room after the doctor told me to tell her he might have to operate again. She had just taken more than anyone could stand for such a long time. She regained her composure later, however, and never lost it again to my knowledge."

". . . I don't remember whether it was Monday or Tuesday that I broke down," Pat said. "I was sitting in the hall with Teddy's parents while a couple of nurses were making their half-hour check of his condition. Suddenly, one came flying out of the room and I thought, *Oh, my God, what happened?* I grabbed the nurse and asked her. She stopped long enough to say, 'There's an irregularity in his vital signs. We're going to call Dr. Ivan to come up and examine him.' Then she turned and ran.

"Dr. Ivan came with two other doctors—I think one was Dr. Shirama, the resident neurosurgeon. They came out looking very grave, and I heard Dr. Ivan tell someone to bring up the encephalograph machine. This really shook me because they had never done that before. Whenever they wanted an EEG, they took Ted to the machine rather than bringing the machine to him. After they took the readings, I was so upset I didn't dare ask Dr. Ivan what was going on. I was afraid of what he'd say. But I had to know, so I asked Ted's father if he'd mind asking. When he came back and said they were considering more surgery, I thought, *God, he can't make it through another operation so soon after the last one,* and then I just came all unglued. I wept and wept right there in the hall. They had to take me into a room to try to calm me down.

" 'Why don't you let me give you something?' the nurse asked.

" 'I don't want anything—I don't want anything,' I said between sobs. 'I want to know what's going on.'

" 'But you've been through so much.'

" 'I know. And I'm being a baby now,' I said.

" 'Well, how about a little ginger ale?'

" 'OK. I'll have something to drink.'

"So she brought me some ginger ale, and of course there was something in it. I didn't know until it was too late. I drained the glass and saw powder at the bottom. It did calm me down without knocking me out, and after a while I went back to the hallway to join Ted's parents. We stayed around all afternoon until one of the nurses suggested we return to the hotel. It was supper time anyhow, and I guess they wanted us all out of there. The nurses promised to phone if there was anything new. I was exhausted and worried, and my nerves were on edge. But I knew sitting around the hallway watching them go in and out with those machines—I think they brought up a portable X-ray, too—wasn't helping any. I couldn't even go into Ted's room. I was afraid of what I'd see.

"Scared as I was, I still got a good night's sleep, and the next morning—Wednesday, probably—my first reaction was relief that nobody had called from the hospital. When I phoned, they told me Teddy was responding well to the medication Dr. Ivan had prescribed and it looked as if they wouldn't have to operate, after all."

Once I pulled out of the critical period, I improved pretty fast. By the end of the week I was walking up and down the corridor. My foot dragged a little, but it was getting better all the time. Dad left to go home on Saturday—he had been there exactly a week. Mom stayed around until the next Thursday. By then my leg was almost normal, although my stride wasn't right yet and I still dragged my foot. My arm continued to feel like a dead weight, but I refused to agree with Dr. Ivan that it wouldn't come back.

A few days before Mom left to go home, she and I were discussing the injury and how it might affect my future.

"Well, for one thing," I said, "I'm going to do all I can to make a comeback with the Bruins."

Mom flared up, then retorted, "You've got to have a hole in your head if you go back to hockey."

For a second neither of us spoke. Then, realizing the

significance of what she had just said, we both burst out laughing.

When Mike Richard got home, I asked him about the arm, and he said, "You've got a 50-50 chance of its coming back."

"I don't give a damn what you say," I said. "I *know* my arm is coming back, and that's all there is to it."

". . . Teddy was in pretty good shape, considering what he had gone through," Dr. Richard said. "I know Dr. Ivan had told him he didn't think the arm would ever get better, and I was inclined to agree. But you never know about these brain things. Besides, Ted Green was the most determined patient I ever had. He had his mind made up that no matter what happened he'd make a complete, fast recovery. I doubted he would ever play hockey again, but he was on skates less than a year after he was hurt, and playing regularly for the Bruins when the 1970–71 season began. That took more than medical science and therapy. It took faith and guts and determination, and Teddy had them all."

They made me hold my arm inside my bathrobe so it wouldn't hang dead the way it had when I first started coming out of that second operation. They didn't want the blood rushing down there, because that would deaden it more. Later, they put it in a sling, which I wore even after I was out of the hospital and back home in Winnipeg.

The Bruins were great. They picked up every tab for every phone call and trip, paid all the medical expenses, and honored to the letter the verbal contract I had made with Charlie Mulcahy. They even sent the same weekly expense money the players got while the team was training at London, Ontario, and they started mailing my salary when the regular season began.

I wasn't allowed to have visitors or take phone calls for about two weeks after the hemorrhage operation. Eddie Johnston called Pat every day to see how I was doing, and as soon as they let me have a phone, he called me. Milt Schmidt also called Pat periodically, and later talked to me regularly.

Pat and I tried to answer some of the mail and telegrams and calls I had received, which was an almost impossible job. But there were two letters I felt we had to write. One was to the Bruin players. The other was to Wayne Maki.

I had ambivalent feelings about Maki—different from any I'd ever had about other opposing hockey players. In our business, you're always having hassles with somebody. That's part of the game. I never dwelled on a clean fight. When it was over it was over, and from then on, the guy I'd fought was just another hockey player. But after a dirty fight, I would think, *I'll get that guy. I don't know when or how, but he's not going to get away with it.* This was a typical reaction. Almost everyone in the NHL has a little grudge in the back of his mind from a previous fight where somebody threw a sneak punch or speared or got a little more rambunctious than necessary.

But I couldn't feel that way about Maki. When I was lying paralyzed in the hospital, I was praying, and my family was praying, and my teammates were praying, and I got letters from people all over Boston saying they were praying and having Masses said for me. If at the same time I was thinking that when I got better I was going to get that SOB Maki, I would really have been a hypocrite. I couldn't generate any hate for the guy, not when I thought about all those prayers. I'd gone after guys who had done much less to me than he had. But I never before associated any of this with praying, which made all the difference.

That was why Pat and I wrote to him, and it was part of the reason we wrote to my own teammates. Of course, we had a million things to thank the Bruin players for: their Mass, their concern, their continued attentiveness, everything they did for us, as individuals and as a group. We mentioned all of that and told them not to worry about me. They had a hockey season to play, and we didn't want my situation to affect their game.

And there was one other thing we didn't want. If they ever had occasion to play against Wayne Maki, we didn't want any of them going after him. We asked them to let the guy alone unless he did something else provocative. We wanted them to forget that he had sent me to the hospital. We wanted them to treat him like any other opposing player—no better, no worse.

We wrote a much shorter letter to Maki. I don't know if he tried to see me at the hospital, or ever asked about me while I was there. I don't know how he felt, but I can imagine. He wouldn't be human if he weren't sorry. All we wrote was that he shouldn't feel too badly about this— it had happened in a hockey game, and hockey isn't for sissies. He had done his best and lost his head. I've lost mine. I know damn few NHL hockey players who haven't at one time or another. The unfortunate result was accidental. We told him so, and said there were no hard feelings on our part, and we meant it.

We sent the letter to Maki, care of Lynn Patrick, the St. Louis Blues' general manager at the time, along with a note to Lynn, asking him to forward it if Maki was elsewhere. Whether Maki got it or not we don't know, because we never heard from him.

". . . By the time the letter arrived, we had farmed Maki out to Buffalo, which then had a minor-league team," Patrick said. "I sent it along to him there."

". . . There was so much mail from the St. Louis Blues with paychecks for the players the Blues had farmed out to us that I really don't know if Maki got the letter or not," said Fred Hunt, a Buffalo official.

There was always a missing link in my mind about the fight. I simply could not understand why I turned away from Maki. About three weeks after my hemorrhage, I was sitting in a chair drinking tea in the hallway outside my room when a cleaning woman came by with a couple of big trash cans on her cart. She'd put the cans on top of some old newspapers before going in to do my room. I looked down, and it was the front page of the Ottawa paper that came out the day after Maki hit me. When I saw the headline, "Ted Green Hurt," I bent down to look more closely. The story was covered up, but I could see several pictures, the first I had seen of the fight. One shot showed Maki with his hands way up in the air, and a second showed him starting to bring his stick down. But neither picture had me turning away, which I must have done because everyone said I did. Under the circumstances, it seemed impossible for me not to have seen that blow coming. I was still looking and trying to figure it out when the cleaning woman came flying out of the room, said, "I'm sorry, Mr. Green," picked up the papers, stuffed them into one of the barrels, and went flying off before I could stop her. Sometime later I saw another set of pictures, one of which showed my feet completely turned away from Maki. Another showed my head turned. Another showed an official with one hand on one of my arms and his other in front of my face. That, apparently, was when I turned away. With all my experience, I should have known better.

Chapter / 5

Instead of one week in the hospital, I spent five. Once I got over the crisis caused by the hemorrhage, my improvement was considered fast by everyone but me. I suppose anybody suffering sudden paralysis gets discouraged and impatient, and I was no exception. I needed therapy from the left side of my face down to the toes on my left foot, and I needed encouragement every minute. Pat showed the most optimism, but I didn't know if she truly felt that way or simply wanted to appear hopeful.

". . . I really didn't know what to think," Pat said. "I wasn't convinced that everything would come back, but I never indicated that to Teddy. I knew he was a stubborn, determined guy who could make things happen if anyone could. But right after he came out of the hemorrhage situation, he needed hope, and I certainly didn't want to say anything that might break his spirit or dull his determination. Although we didn't talk much about it, we both thought a lot about hockey. I'm sure Teddy was convinced he could play again. Personally, I was sure he wouldn't. I would have settled for minimum paralysis. I never dreamed he'd make it all the way back to the Bruins. I doubt if anyone else did either."

". . . Before the hemorrhage, I thought he'd play hockey again," said Dr. Richard. "But the hemorrhage caused so much additional damage I couldn't imagine him playing."

". . . I didn't know anything about hockey until I met Mr. Green," said his physiotherapist, Mrs. Winifred Platt. Brought up on the island of Malta, she is married to a Canadian. Young, slight, vivacious, with brown hair and huge brown eyes, she was warm and understanding, but had an unmistakable air of formality. As long as she worked with Green, she was "Mrs. Platt" to him and he was "Mr. Green" to her.

"He was an outstandingly good patient," she said. "He worked as hard as anyone I've ever seen. I wasn't sure his arm would come back. After meeting him, I watched a couple of hockey games on television, and from what I saw, there seemed to me no hope of Mr. Green ever playing again. These men skated too fast, were too clever with the sticks they used, and had amazingly quick reflexes. Even if everything came back for Mr. Green, I didn't see how he could expect to play. I thought he'd have trouble with skating alone, and doing all the other things necessary for a professional hockey player seemed far beyond his capacities."

Mama Schwartz, my favorite nurse, a motherly German woman who always had a smile on her face and a little wisecrack on her lips, told me time and again that everything was going to be fine. The other nurses were much the same way, except I didn't always believe them. Mama Schwartz could make me believe anything. Whenever she told me in her hearty, warm manner that I'd come back all the way, she made my day.

It had been a bad mistake to ask Dr. Ivan to level with me; I don't think he would have done so if I hadn't insisted.

("I wouldn't have," Dr. Ivan said. "I hate to tell a patient bad news, because his morale is most important in the difficult process of trying to bring him back. Some people would just give up, and I certainly didn't want to say anything that might make Mr. Green do that. But his strength of character was as powerful as his physical strength, and I don't think anything I said would have changed his outlook. He wanted to know what I thought, and I told him. To me, the fact that his arm and hand and fingers came back was a surprise, and that he could play professional hockey again was nothing short of a miracle.")

Dr. Ivan's opinion was one of the things that plunged me into deep depression from time to time. Sometimes I lay alone during the night and wept, and sometimes I wept during the day when I wasn't alone. I wanted so badly to be normal, to come back—and to play hockey. I didn't care about pain or hard work or setbacks or obstacles obvious to everyone around me. I didn't want to think anything was insurmountable. But then I'd recall those words of Dr. Ivan, a fine, highly respected neurosurgeon: *In my opinion, your left arm won't come back.* I didn't want to believe him—I couldn't believe him—yet there were times I was afraid he might be right.

Then too, there was Mike Richard with his "50-50 chance." Mike and I had a wonderful relationship. He was close to my age, a friend, a man who could make everything sound funny even when it was not.

Like the time, just before I left the hospital, when he told me to wear a helmet playing hockey. Then, hockey, especially NHL hockey, seemed a virtual impossibility. My arm was in a sling. My face was still turned down. My speech wasn't right. There was no way anyone except me could expect I'd play professional hockey again. But Mike, who I'm sure didn't believe I could make it back, talked as if he did. One thing he told me was to wear a helmet when I started playing again.

"How the hell can I wear a helmet?" I said. "The thing would drive me nuts."

"You'd be nuts if you didn't," he said. "After all, it would be pretty silly if somebody belted you on the left side of your head. How would you like to go through this business all over again?"

"Lightning won't strike twice in the same place," I said. "That wouldn't be the same place," he answered. "It would be in the opposite place."

While I appreciated everyone's help and encouragement, the one person who taught me the most about myself was Mrs. Platt. She made me understand what I had to do in order to return all the way. She explained that you have many brain cells controlling the same part of the body, but that some are dormant and never used. This doesn't mean they can't be used. They're dormant simply because other cells normally do the work. When the active cells are destroyed, you have to develop these dormant cells. And unless they, too, are damaged, they can take over for the cells you've lost.

"Knowing these dormant cells are there," she said, "you must concentrate on putting them to use. The results can be very gratifying."

Early in those last two weeks in the hospital, I lay in bed and concentrated on my shoulder. The reason I worked on it was that Mrs. Platt told me that when you have brain damage, the first affected part of your body (in my case, my left hand) is the last part to come back, and what is affected last comes back first. Except for my leg, which came around quickly and completely within ten days after the hemorrhage operation, my shoulder had been the last to go.

I had never before gone into such deep concentration, blocking everything else out of my mind. I guess it was a form of self-hypnosis. I just lay there and thought, *Brain to shoulder—brain to shoulder—brain to shoulder.* Whatever dormant part of my brain that might control it was the part I tried to wake up, to put to use so my shoulder would move. Until I could do that I wouldn't be able to move any other part of my arm.

About six o'clock one morning while lying in bed unable to sleep, I lost myself concentrating on the shoulder. Finally, still thinking only about that, I lifted my limp left arm with my good right hand and moved it straight up over my head. When I then tried to move the left arm, the strangest feeling came over me, and I thought, *It's going to work—it's going to work!* And, sure enough, my whole arm, propelled by my shoulder, actually moved all by itself about three inches, just enough so that when it fell, it came down on my chest instead of above my head, where it had been when I started.

I was so overcome I cried like a baby right there in the hospital bed. And, even though I couldn't move it again right away, the tears kept running down my cheeks, for I knew if I'd done it once I would be able to do it again sooner or later. I must have cried five minutes before I stopped. And when the nurse came in, I yelled, "I moved my shoulder—I moved it—I moved it!"

"Wonderful," she said.

"Let me show you."

Again, I used my good arm to bring the bad one up over

my head, and again it didn't work. But I still was tickled pink.

"I'll do it before the day's over," I said.

"I'm sure you will," she encouraged.

That afternoon, while Pat was there, I said, "Honey, look what I can do."

As she stood by the bed and watched me, I raised my bad arm with my good and, as I concentrated on that dormant brain cell that could control the left shoulder, I managed to move my shoulder again, just as I had done early in the morning. It went no more than three inches. Enough, because my arm fell on my chest. I laughed and said, "See? See? If I can do that, I can do anything."

Pat was as happy as I, and so was Mrs. Platt, even though she must have seen such things happen hundreds of times. She praised me for my determination and concentration, then said, "Now, don't forget, Mr. Green, you've got the rest of that arm and the hand and the fingers to move. They'll come next. You'll see."

She took me to the hospital gym, where she worked with my hand and wrist. I got down on my knees, put my right hand flat on the floor, and she did the same with my left, since I couldn't move it myself. While I moved my right arm, she worked with my left and helped me maneuver up and down, up and down, in a series of push-ups. I was amazed at her physical strength. Thin and slight as she was, she could still move the whole left side of my body, pulling it up, letting it down, pulling it up, letting it down. This strengthened my shoulder and the muscle in back of my arm, and helped the hand, which was still inert.

My own shoulder movements began to improve within 24 hours after I had first moved it from above my head. One day when Mike Richard came in, I said, "Put my left arm up in the air." When he had done that, I said, "Now push it down." I watched a look of surprise come over his face when he found he couldn't do it because my tricep muscle was now strong enough to hold him back.

"You're growing almost as strong as Teddy Green," he intoned.

While Mrs. Platt was optimistic about my arm, she wasn't so sure about the hand and fingers. "I don't know if we can do anything with your hand or not, Mr. Green," she said. "Start concentrating on it and keep working at it."

In bed that night, I began thinking, *Brain to fingers*, and for days I went into more deep concentration. One morning about a week before I left the hospital, there was a tiny flicker of the second finger on my left hand. I was so excited I got out of bed and ran across the corridor to see the guy in that room, a young fellow named Jerry Heath. I started ranting and raving that my finger was moving. I put my hand on his bed tray and told him to watch. It took five minutes, but then the same finger moved again. Jerry grinned and said, "Teddy, you're getting it—you're getting it!"

In a day or two I could move all but the thumb, which

continued to stick out stiffly. Except for my speech, it was the only thing that hadn't come back before the hemorrhage, and I knew it would give me trouble.

One morning Pat came into the room, saw I was concentrating, and didn't even greet me. She simply stood at the foot of the bed watching my thumb. When she saw it flicker, she let out a yelp, and the two of us jumped around the room like maniacs.

But I continued to have periods of deep depression when I thought of all the things my family might have to do for me—dress me, help me to the bathroom, sometimes feed me. I thought about the good times we'd always had in the past and wondered whether we could ever have such times again. I thought what a burden I'd be on everyone in the family—not just Pat, but my parents, my brothers, and, when they were older, my children. I wondered how I could make a living. Even though the Bruins honored our verbal agreement, that would be only for three years, and what would I do then? Hockey was the only thing I knew, the only profession I had ever had.

I got over all these feelings in the therapy gym one day when I was down there with Mrs. Platt. While I was lying on a mat doing some exercises under her supervision, they brought in a young fellow in truly terrible shape. He had lost coordination in all four limbs, and his speech was so bad you couldn't understand him at all. When they laid him on the mat beside me, he turned his head and tried to say "hi," but even that didn't come out right. Then he said something that sounded like "hockey" and smiled. I realized he was a fan who knew about me and apparently had been told about my injury. I wanted to talk to him, to react in some way that would give him a little lift, but I felt so terribly sorry for him that I got all choked up, and Mrs. Platt had to move me. I learned he had been a brilliant college student, but was so badly injured in an automobile accident they didn't know what, if anything, they could do for him—that he might be helpless the rest of his life.

From then on, I never again felt sorry for myself, for here was a guy whose whole life had been smashed to bits. After that, whenever I met him in therapy, I talked hockey to him, telling him all about the Bruins and the other NHL clubs. His smile more than made up for the fact that his speech was gibberish. I've often wondered what happened to him. I hope he regained some of what he had lost—enough, at least, to allow him to do things for himself.

During my last week in the hospital, Mike Richard suggested that I leave the place for a short period to get accustomed to fresh air and to use my legs outdoors so I wouldn't feel faint on the trip home. Pat helped me dress, and the nurses put a sling on my left arm to hold it up. Mama Schwartz walked us to the front door, and for the first time since I was hurt, I saw the hospital from the outside.

It was a long, rambling series of brick buildings in the

heart of Ottawa's French Canadian district, on Bruyere Street. And the main entrance was a block from the opposite end of Parliament Park, where most of the government buildings as well as the Chateau Laurier Hotel were. Practically all the signs in the area were in French, including shop and street names, and almost everyone we passed was speaking French. We turned to the right after leaving the hospital and, arm in arm, started slowly toward the park, enjoying the bright sunshine that cut through the crisp autumn air. We stopped at one little store, bought some candy, then crossed the street, sat on some stone steps leading down to the bank of a narrow river, and sort of lost ourselves. Time and the whole world stopped as we munched the candy and talked about whatever came into our heads. The sheer enjoyment of being outdoors together on such a glorious day completely overwhelmed us. Every so often we looked across the river at the great green expanse of the park, with the capital buildings in the distance. I remember thinking what a beautiful sight it was and how much we'd have enjoyed being there under other circumstances. And I remember asking Pat how far we were from the other end of the park and the hospital. She answered, "A long way, honey. It's a good twenty-minute walk from the Chateau."

After a while we stood up and went into a little French restaurant where we ate chips, drank soda, and talked some more. As we left we nearly ran into Mama Schwartz hurrying along the street, a worried look on her face.

When she saw us, she said in her heavy German accent, "Do you know how long you've been gone? Over an hour! You weren't supposed to be out more than half that time. We've been frightened to death something had happened." Then she broke into a big smile. "I bet you had a good time," she said.

"A wonderful time," I replied. "In fact, one of the best times I've had in my life."

Late that week Mike Richard took us over to his home in Hull, Quebec, on the other side of the river from Ottawa. He had a most attractive layout, including a spacious house, a barn, and other out-buildings, as well as some animals, the most impressive of which were two sleek colts. While we were there, his sister and brother-in-law, Sue and Guy Demers, dropped in. After kidding me about my bald head (little spikes of hair were beginning to sprout), they told me that, like Mike, they were ardent fans of the Canadiens. Still, they asked me to pose for pictures, with a cat peeking out of my sling. Later, Mike drove us back to the hospital.

Either that day or the next, a couple of men identifying themselves as plainclothesmen from the police department asked to see me. When they came into the room one said, "Do you want to press charges against Wayne Maki?"

"No," I said.

"He hit you from behind, injured you very badly, and you probably have a strong case against him."

"It happened in a hockey game and could have happened to anyone. I definitely don't want to press charges."

They said OK and walked out, but that wasn't the last of it. The day before Pat and I went home to Winnipeg, Clarence Campbell, president of the National Hockey League, came to Ottawa to conduct an investigation of his own. I didn't know it at the time, but the Crown was already preparing a case against Maki and me, charging us both with assault with attempt to injure. I guess it was an unprecedented action, because the only cases involving professional hockey games had been civil actions between players and fans. This was the first time two players were accused of criminal action arising from something that happened between them in a game. I understood very few of the ramifications, and to this day I'm not sure exactly what they were or precisely why authorities had singled out Maki and me for prosecution. Our hassle had been a typical hockey fight. The only thing that distinguished it from many others was I'd been badly hurt.

Mr. Campbell's hearing was held in the offices of Edward S. Houston, an Ottawa lawyer the Bruins had engaged to represent me. Mr. Campbell had asked that all the principals in the case be present, including Bruins' and Blues' officials, the game's referee and linesmen, several other witnesses, Wayne Maki, and me. Whether Mr. Campbell checked with the hospital to see if I could stand what might become an ordeal, I don't know; but it didn't matter because by then I had already taken several more walks outdoors with Pat. The only trouble was, I tired very easily.

On the morning of the hearing, just as Pat was finishing breakfast in the coffee shop of the Chateau, Lynn Patrick, then the Blues' general manager, accompanied by a young man Pat didn't recognize, came in and sat down at the table beside her. Pat knew Lynn, since he'd been the Bruins' general manager in my early years with them, so she stopped on her way out to greet him. They exchanged a few pleasantries, then Pat left to come to the hospital for me. Only after she was outside did she realize that the guy with Patrick must have been Maki. Lynn hadn't introduced her.

("I didn't recognize Pat at first," Patrick said. "I hadn't seen her for several years, and had never known any of the hockey wives well. However, as soon as she spoke, I realized who she was, and, frankly, I didn't know what to do. Maki was with me, but I was too embarrassed to introduce them. After she left, I said, 'Wayne, that's Teddy Green's wife,' and he answered, 'Oh, is it?' That was the only mention of the incident by either of us.")

I wouldn't have minded the hearing if I could have testified and then left, but Campbell insisted I stay longer. The first time I saw Maki since the fight was in Houston's office. I wasn't embarrassed, but I think he was, or maybe just sorry. He saw me paralyzed and bald-headed, with a big ugly scar, my left arm in a sling, my face over to one side, and my speech still garbled. We didn't talk much.

Just shook hands and exchanged "hi's" or some such thing. Campbell asked me to testify first. I shouldn't have said anything because I really didn't know what had happened. But I mumbled something—I'm not sure what—and the longer I tried to talk, the wearier I got. The room was hot and I wasn't myself. The nurses were calling Pat, who was in another room of the lawyer's suite, saying we should leave; except Mr. Campbell wanted me to stay. Ever since the hemorrhage, I'd never been able to go more than a couple of hours before falling asleep, but even after I finished talking, they wouldn't let me go. So there I sat, dog-tired and boiling hot, almost until the last gun was fired.

I had to listen to Maki's testimony, but I really didn't give a damn what he said. All I remember was that he claimed he had no recollection of spearing me. I knew he *had* speared me, but I was just too tired to mention it. We must have been there two hours before somebody knocked on the door and said it was absolutely essential that I get back to the hospital. I don't think Mr. Campbell was too happy about my leaving, but I don't think he should have made me go in the first place. I wasn't prepared mentally or physically either to give or to rebut any testimony. I just wanted to sleep.

". . . I knew Green was in bad shape, but the hospital people said he had been taking walks and could probably stand the hearing," Campbell said. "He was going home the next day, and it was the only chance I had to get everyone together. Once there, I felt Green should hear Maki's side so he could defend himself if he wanted to. However, when he became so tired that it was obvious he couldn't contribute anything more to the hearing, I was perfectly willing to let him leave.

"I've always held that civil authority must take precedence over the league's, and there was a criminal suit pending against both Green and Maki at the time of the hearing in Ottawa. When violations of criminal or civil law are involved, everyone must make way for it, and anyone assuming to replace it is subject to contempt of court. That's why I waited so long to make a decision.

"The charge against both players of assault with intent to injure was grossly discriminatory. The only previous suits we'd ever had involved players and fans, but this involved only players. I kept in close touch with the police, and there was every reason to believe they would drop the charges.

"Eventually, in separate trials, Maki and Green were each acquitted. I then suspended both without pay, Green for 13 games and Maki for 30 days. In Green's case the suspension was technical because he didn't play at all that year. It cost him more money, however, because he earned much more than Maki. In order to clear him of future obligations to the league, the Bruins reactivated him for the last 13 games of the regular season, and his pay was withheld for those games.

"I am satisfied of two points. From the testimony, I am

convinced Maki did spear Green. From the pictures, I am convinced Maki's blow ricocheted off Green's stick before it hit Green on the head, causing his injury."

While I remember nothing about being hit, everything I've been told points to the certainty that Maki hit me squarely on the head. I doubt I would have been as severely hurt if his stick had ricocheted off mine first. One of the pictures is very deceiving. It seems to show Maki's stick hitting mine, which was high, but it shows us facing each other. The picture actually captured the aftereffect of the blow, when, stunned by Maki's stick, mine came up by reflex action as I started going down.

I could have done very nicely without that damn hearing. There was no point to it. Nothing I said added to what was already known. And the whole thing was so tiresome that even if I had been healthy it would probably have put me to sleep.

The next day we flew home.

Chapter / 6

I know of few thrills greater than getting out after a long stay in the hospital, yet you sometimes leave with a touch of regret. At first you're an utter stranger, especially if you've never before been in the city where the hospital is located. But as days and weeks go on, you make new friends—more than friends, I suppose, for some help you with your most intimate daily habits and necessities.

I made good friends at the Ottawa General Hospital. The best, of course, was Dr. Mike Richard, with whom I remain close to this day. Mama Schwartz, the nurse who spent so much time helping and encouraging me, was more like a jolly, endearing relative. Mrs. Platt, Dr. Ivan, Nurse Margaret Kelly—all gave me hope, and left their marks of true friendship on Pat and me.

I was no stranger to hospitals. In 1966 and 1967 I was in and out of them for months at a time with knee problems, and through the years I've been hospitalized with other injuries. I made friends at some, but none quite like the people at Ottawa. I spent more than a month in that predominantly French hospital. Although Pat, her mother, and my mother (all French Canadians, who speak English with a French accent) are fluent in French, and I was born and raised in a bilingual community, my French is terrible and I had never felt the impact of French Canadian ways as shown in the Ottawa General Hospital. I'll never forget the warmth and interest those people took in me.

Dr. Richard was a Canadian of French extraction, as were most of my nurses. There were others, however, who were not French, had no French blood, yet spoke with pronounced accents of their own; and they remain vivid in my mind. Mrs. Platt, a Maltese, had a strong British stress. Dr. Ivan, despite his excellent English, was a Hungarian who retained his inflection. Mama Schwartz, who left a deeper imprint on Pat and me than anyone else except Mike Richard, spoke in the gutteral tones of her native Germany.

We were leaving friends. Yet neither Pat nor I had seen anyone except my parents for all those weeks, and we were anxious to get home. We both badly missed our three kids, to whom we spoke on the phone occasionally, but since Karen, the eldest, was only five, it was hard to hold their attention long. One of the few times I saw Pat as upset as she had been after my hemorrhage was when she talked to Brian, our youngest, and thought it was Christopher. With tears in her eyes she turned to me and said, "We've been away so long I can't even recognize the baby's voice. In just these few weeks he's changed that much."

I looked forward to seeing my two brothers. The three of us are as close as any brothers I know. Tony is only eleven months older than I, and Ken just a year younger. Tony was a good athlete, and we played various sports together. Ken might have played too, except for polio, which affected his leg somewhat, although he has no limp today.

So, despite the friends we made in Ottawa, we were happy to leave. Besides, I knew I'd be back for periodic examinations and an eventual operation to cover the hole in my skull, now protected merely by a thin layer of skin. Beneath that was only the dura—the brain covering—which meant I had to be very careful. Mike told me to wear something on my head at all times to reinforce the spot where the wound had been.

Once settled on the airplane from Ottawa to Winnipeg, I turned to Pat and said, "Y'know, honey, I did a lot of thinking while I was in the hospital. And there's one thing that really bugged me, and still does."

"What's that?" she asked.

"What in hell do you suppose got into me that I turned away from Maki before the fight was over?"

She smiled a sad sort of smile and said, "Teddy—Teddy—what's done is done. The world is full of people who did the wrong thing at the wrong time with even more disastrous results. Don't let this bug you. Just stop thinking about it. You made a mistake. You paid for it. Now forget it."

I didn't forget, and haven't, but I've never again discussed it at any length with Pat. We had far happier things to talk about on that trip home—the people in Ottawa, the family, our house in St. Boniface, and the grand reunion we'd have with our children there.

We talked very little about hockey. Pat knew me well enough to understand that if there was any possible way I could play again, I would. She also knew, as I did, that I had a long, long way to go. We took this trip the day after the Campbell hearing, and I was in exactly the same shape as I'd been then. My face was twisted, my speech slurred, my left arm in a sling. I could move my fingers, but movement is a long way from dexterity, and it would be months before I reached that stage. My fingers had the stiffness of a puppet's. I couldn't sign my name, nor did I have any real feeling in the extremities. To this day, the tips of my left fingers are almost insensitive. I carry small items such as change in my right pocket instead of my left, where I used to carry them, because I can't tell one coin from another except with the fingers of my right hand. For more than a year I couldn't lift small metal objects off a flat surface with my left hand, although I do this pretty well now. My writing has come back, but I must grip a pen or pencil very tightly, which makes autographing something of a chore because the effort quickly tires my fingers. However, when people ask for my autograph I like to oblige, especially on the way back and forth between the ice and the locker room. That's where the most faithful fans are. And on a few occasions I've signed as many as 200 autographs at a time.

My speech gradually improved to a point where I could be easily understood, then reached a plateau where it remained for months. It was over a year before I could give a talk to a large group. Even now my speech slips back to where it was after my injury when I'm excited, upset, or emotional. I always had a tendency to talk too fast and slur my words. That became accentuated unless I forced myself to concentrate on talking, just as I'd concentrated on all the other things that had to be done while I was in the hospital.

I'm much more openly emotional now than I ever was before. Part of this may be a residual of the original injury. But I think it's also due to the kindness and concern I found in others. I got so much help from so many people while I was recovering that I realize now that warmth and compassion are basic human characteristics. I guess this is something we all learn when we brush close to death or permanent disability. Today I realize, too, that crying is not just for babies. It's no crime for a grown man to cry when moved, nor is it anything to be ashamed of. Before I was hurt I fought off any outward signs of emotion. Now

I let those feelings show. I can't help it. It has become as natural to me as breathing.

Pat and I discussed all these things as we traveled home to Winnipeg from Ottawa that happy day I left the hospital. And while studiously avoiding the subject of hockey, we talked of the future in terms of what we might do if I couldn't make it back to the Bruins. We have always loved the out-of-doors, and central Canada is naturally beautiful. We talked of the possibility of selling our house and buying a ranch, where we could live and work outdoors even if I continued to be handicapped with a gimpy left arm.

While that sounded ideal, there was the problem of being too far away from the family, both Pat's and mine, and of finding good schools for the children. Somewhat to my surprise, Pat pulled out a set of plans for a city house she had found in the home section of a Sunday newspaper while we were in Ottawa. It was beautifully laid out, with everything we'd ever want or need. Maybe for Pat it was a sort of dream house, and thinking and planning about it gave her something to get her mind off me while I was in the hospital.

The ranch or the dream house sounded great, almost like a perpetual vacation. Yet deep in our hearts we knew it wouldn't be great for me; I love hockey too much to give it up before I have to.

"... As a matter of fact," Pat said, "none of us, including Teddy's brothers, who have always been proud of his success, were crazy about his going back to hockey, even if he could. We all were acutely aware of the danger of another injury. But after Teddy and I got home we realized the ranch idea wouldn't work, for we'd have to live too far from town. I kept talking about the dream house for months though, because, despite Teddy's physical improvement, hockey still appeared miles away. He could function, but there seemed no chance of his regaining the fine coordination and reflex action essential to an NHL hockey player. I never mentioned that, of course, but I did manage to get him to go with me looking at possible home sites around Winnipeg. We even found something so promising we seriously considered buying it, but Teddy kept thinking up excuses not to—every excuse but the one closest to his heart, that maybe he *could* make it back and then we'd be stuck with an expensive piece of property we might not build on for years. He never mentioned it, but there was another very practical problem. If he didn't make it back, we'd never in the world be able to swing the cost of the kind of house we wanted to build.

"I guess in a sense we were playing games," Pat went on. "I would lead the conversation into ranches and houses and other such things, but I knew what hockey meant to Teddy, and I knew his pride wouldn't permit him to give it up without a fight. I knew how hard he would fight to get back. And because he wanted it so badly, I wanted it for him. That was why I later encouraged him to keep trying when he went into deep depressions over the apparent hopelessness of his ever playing hockey again. These depressions were fundamentally no different from those he had at the hospital. Only the objectives were different. At Ottawa he fretted over his failure to move a finger or to speak clearly or to lift his arm high enough. At Winnipeg he fretted over his failure to develop strength and reflex action and good coordination fast enough for the next hockey season.

"I've been a hockey fan ever since we were married in April 1963. I miss very few Boston games at home—only if one of the kids is sick or something else important interferes. I had seen Teddy hurt a few times—never as badly as at Ottawa—and I had lived with him through two rough years while his knees were healing. But I had never worried about him. I knew he could take care of himself, and I wasn't afraid for him.

"But now," she added, "I kept thinking, *If he makes it back, can I ever again be comfortable watching him play? Can I ever relax in the stands when he's on the ice? Can I ever again see him fall without feeling my heart leap and my back go cold with fear?* Yet I knew there was only one choice for me. If anybody could come back from such an injury, it was Teddy. And no one wanted to come back more than he. How could I do or say anything to discourage him? I couldn't cure him, or go through the agony of exercises and work and disappointments for him—only he could do that. So I must encourage him: keep telling him not to give up, keep watching for every little improvement in his condition and rejoice with him in it. Above all, I must never give him even a hint of how I really felt—that it would be all right with me if he never again put on a pair of skates, or held a hockey stick, or rushed the puck across an opposing blue line. I won't say I wanted him to quit. I wanted him to do what he wanted. But if he decided he couldn't do it, that it was beyond human endurance, I wouldn't have been unhappy.

"Hockey paid him well, but no amount of money could make up for what he had been through or what he might some day have to go through again. We both came from working families. We had been comfortable growing up, but never wealthy. My father is a custom tailor. Teddy, whose father is with the railroad, was in just about the same financial bracket. We lived in the same neighborhood, where everyone was pretty much in the same boat. The houses were modest and neat. They were not the homes of rich people. Nobody among our Winnipeg friends made the kind of money Teddy earned playing hockey. Our parents had managed on a great deal less. And I knew we'd manage, too, if he couldn't play. We would simply return to the less affluent life we both knew so well.

"I truly couldn't imagine him making it back to the Bruins. That was too much to expect. But I still had my mind set to do everything I could to help him. What he wanted was all that counted with me. That was why on the trip home we deliberately avoided the real subject uppermost in our minds: Could he ever play NHL hockey again? And if so, should he?

"My answer to the last question had to be yes. It couldn't have been anything else."

All through the flight home I squeezed a rubber ball Mrs. Platt had given me. I knew I'd be doing things like that for months, because my fingers would be the last to come back. I knew, too, that I'd be doing other exercises, some recommended by Mrs. Platt, others to develop my strength and wind and reflexes. With hockey my eventual goal, my immediate aim had to be body-building. And it would be a long uphill battle.

The nearer we got to Winnipeg the more excited I became. Pat was going through the same thing, for she fell silent when the pilot announced we were starting the descent to the airport. We sat quietly, holding hands—my good right and her left—looking forward to the most wonderful family reunion we had ever known. In minutes we would be home—home from the fear and doubt and physical setbacks of hospital life. I had been in hospitals longer, but never with anything as serious. We'd had family reunions before, but never after such an ordeal. Nearly five weeks is a long time to be away from small children.

Mom and Dad and my brother Tony met us at the airport. They didn't bring the kids because they rightly figured that seeing the children and everyone else too would be more excitement than was good for me. Kenny, my younger brother, was at work (he's a fireman in St. Boniface). When I caught sight of Tony, I decided to give him a hug. After greeting my folks, I shook his hand, then put my good arm around him and squeezed him hard, a gesture he returned with both arms. This was a rare display of affection, for, close as we are, we were never very demonstrative about our feelings for each other.

My folks and Tony each had brought a car. Pat went home to our house with my parents, since the children were there. I asked Tony to take me to the firehouse in St. Boniface. When we arrived we both got out of the car, and while I waited, Tony went in for Kenny. He came out and we greeted each other just as Tony and I had. For a second or two, as the three of us stood together beside Tony's car, I thought we were all going to burst into tears, but we managed not to. Yet I think in that moment we felt as close as we ever had in our lives.

". . . There wasn't any question about our emotionalism," Tony said later. "Kenny and I were used to having Ted away for long periods, since he had been in pro hockey 10 years. But we always looked forward to his coming home so the three of us could do things together. This time we had gone through days when we weren't sure we'd ever be together again, and weeks when we thought Ted's handicaps might be too severe for him to hunt or fish or play golf with us. Kenny and I had always missed

Ted during the hockey season, but at least we knew he'd be home later. This time we weren't so sure.

"As we stood there in front of Kenny's firehouse, we all seemed to know instinctively that, even though Ted had been through a lot and still had a long way to go, those happy days weren't over. With God's help and good luck, they wouldn't be for a long time."

Tony shook his head and added, "I'd love to see him quit hockey. But I know Teddy. This is his bread and butter. And this is what he likes doing. He's put up with so much, though. How much more can he take?"

Odd, about that ugly scar of mine. Months later, both my brothers mentioned that the sight of it scared them almost as much as the sling on my arm and my twisted face. I can't say I blame them. The night I got home, Don Whitman, a sports announcer in Winnipeg, interviewed me on film. When I saw the pictures on television the next day, I didn't think I looked too good either, largely because I was still practically bald and you could see the scar.

Tony drove me home from the firehouse. When we arrived, the kids were clutching at Pat, whom I'm sure they had missed more than they missed me. They were too young to know what had happened, and the boys didn't even seem to recognize me, although Karen did. She kissed me sort of shyly and went back to her mother. I had been gone several weeks longer than Pat and obviously looked different from the daddy they had last seen. Still, the boys let me kiss them before they, too, turned back to Pat. They weren't nearly as excited as I, and I couldn't expect them to be.

Suddenly, I felt dead tired. Mother had left my favorite meal in the oven for me—macaroni and cheese homestyle—but I couldn't each much of it. All I wanted to do was sleep. The trip from Ottawa, the excitement of seeing everybody, the emotional impact of getting home, had exhausted me. Pat helped me undress and get into bed, and I slept for hours.

Strange things kept happening to me during the next weeks. My eyes sometimes played tricks. There was nothing basically wrong with them, but I'd had some double vision and occasional foggy vision in the hospital, a condition the doctors told me would last for some time. My peripheral vision wasn't too good either, but that, too, sometimes comes with brain damage and gets better in time. I think a good deal of my fatigue was due to my eyes tiring, because often the first sign of exhaustion was either a headache or misty or double vision. I was used to all this, but I never thought there was anything wrong with my ears until Sunday, when we went to my parents' house for dinner. We were eating in the kitchen when the phone rang—or at least I thought it rang. I went into the hallway to answer it, but all I heard was a dial tone.

When I went back to the kitchen, everyone—Pat, my

parents, my brothers, even Karen, I guess—looked at me as if I was nuts. I suddenly burst out laughing because the whole thing struck me as damned funny. Everyone else laughed, too. The same thing happened at my own house a few weeks later. I could have sworn the phone rang, but when I answered, all I got was the dial tone.

("I remember those incidents," Pat said. "They didn't worry me because Mike Richard had told us both there was no way of anticipating the aftermaths of a brain injury. All he ever wanted us to tell him was if Teddy had a full-scale seizure, which remained a definite possibility.")

Quite aware of the possibility of seizures, I never drove alone even after I was physically able to do so. I took dilantin, an anticonvulsion drug doctors often prescribe for epileptics, and it worked well. I had a couple of abortive seizures (momentary blackouts that don't develop into full-scale convulsions), but nothing serious enough to call Mike Richard. He had told me not to worry about those, that I might have a few but the dilantin should keep them from building up into anything worse, as, indeed, it did.

We took all sorts of little precautions. There was a cabinet with a sharp corner near the telephone where Pat and I had bumped our heads innumerable times; she put a thick sponge over it. She got me a baseball batting helmet, which I was supposed to wear until my skull was closed. I got real smart about a week after arriving home when I went out with George Hague, my partner in a driving range, to help him close it for the winter. George, who is

Tony and me with Buddy.

Our St. Boniface Juvenile team. I was fourteen at the time; and you'll find me in the back row.

A first year Junior with the St. Boniface Canadiens.

UPI

UPI

After Maki speared me, I retaliated by chopping him on the shoulder with my stick. He then lowered the boom on me. And that was it.

UPI

Here it is again from across the the rink. I've just chopped Maki. He rises. The linesman intervenes; and I turn away (notice my skates here). Maki's stick strikes me, causing mine to go up reflexively.

All photos by Ted Grant, Jr.

OPPOSITE TOP: Our outing at Mike's. From the left: Pat, Mike Richard, Sue Demers, the patient, and Margaret Richard.

OPPOSITE BOTTOM: Leaving Ottawa General for good.

RIGHT: With a friend. November 1969. As you can see, the left side of my face is still noticeably affected.

BELOW: I'll never forget Harry Sinden telling me to climb aboard for this ride with Eddie Westfall, Phil Esposito, Johnny Bucyk, and the Stanley Cup.

Boston Globe

Working out at the Colonial Hilton Health Club, under the watchful eye of Gene Berde

A thoughtful moment at training camp. September 1970.

BELOW: With Bobby and "Turk" in London, Ontario.

Boris Spremo

Camilla Smith

Brian and Chris.

Camilla Smith

ABOVE: Pat and ⬛ Mom and Dad.

RIGHT: My team ⬛ appraise a shot from the blue line.

BELOW: E. J. and I combine to block this effort by Jean Ratelle of the Rangers. That's Rod Gilbert in the background.

Dan Baliotti

UPI

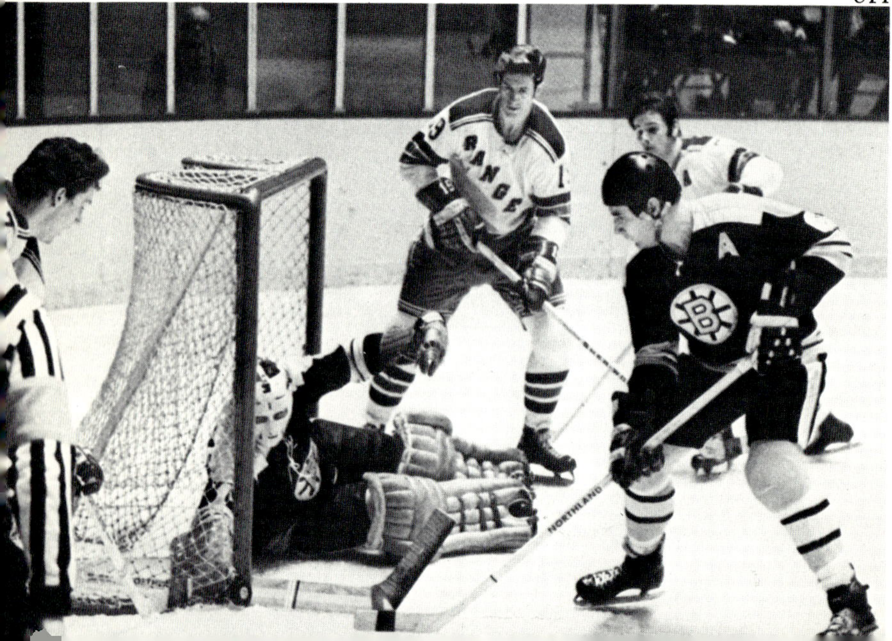

Jerry Buckley

Boarding a Penguin.

Up ice against Vancouver.

Boston Globe

A wry moment.

"Booster Night," November 1970, to prepare for my night at the Garden. Back row, left to right: Eddie Johnston, Gerry Cheevers, Wayne Carleton, Don Awrey, Eddie Westfall, Billy Speers, Don Marcotte, Coach Tom Johnson, Wayne Cashman. Front row, left to right: Ken Hodge, Ted and Pat Green, Danny Shock, Ace Bailey, Bobby Orr.

Dan Baliotti

Boston Globe

Jerry Buckley

ABOVE: Up ice again. This time in pursuit of Chicago's Cliff Koroll.

Jerry Buckley

ABOVE: Here it's Jean Beliveau of Montreal in pursuit. And he was quite a pursuer.

RIGHT: Karen, Brian, and Chris turn out for the Bruins Christmas party. December 1970.

Gerry Cheevers and I manage to protect the goal against Montreal's little Henri Richard.

All photos by Jerry Buckley

Jerry Buckley

ABOVE: E. J. and Dum-Dum at the Topsfield Golf and Country Club. August 1971.

Dan Baliotti

Though I had a lump in my throat, Pat and I were among friends.

in his fifties, is my closest friend in Winnipeg outside of my brothers. When we reached the range, about two miles from my house, I left the helmet in the car and went over to a five-foot-high shed. George asked me to pass him a board, and when I straightened up I hit my head on a sharp corner, about one inch above my right ear and less than an inch below the open skull. It knocked me down and drew a little blood, but I was more scared than hurt. That was the last time I went out without the helmet.

Except for short automobile rides, I rarely left the house at all my first few weeks home. I felt tired all that time, especially after lunch. By one o'clock my head would start aching and my vision blurring, so Pat would help me undress and get into bed. I'd then sleep anywhere from an hour and a half to three hours, then wake up fairly refreshed but still not feeling like doing much.

It was months before I could do a reasonable job of dressing myself, and in those early days at home Pat would have to help me with almost everything. My worst problem was with buttons, because I couldn't use my left hand and couldn't train the right. Even after I returned to the Bruins I needed help with my shirt. I didn't want Coach Tom Johnson or any of the others to know about this. I was afraid they would think I was too tired to play, and I wouldn't get all the ice time I needed. Usually Eddie Johnston helped me. His locker was in a corner, near the equipment room, so I'd go over quietly and say, "Hey, don't let anyone see you, but button me up, will you?"

Sometimes Dan Canney or Frosty Foristall would help me. They were the only others I ever asked.

The terrible fatigue that plagued me in Winnipeg didn't begin to ease until just before Pat and I flew to Ottawa for a checkup. By then my arm was somewhat improved, but not my fingers. Pat had to go with me—I couldn't travel alone because of a possible seizure, and I wanted her with me anyhow. We went in mid-November, and planned to go on to Boston if I felt up to the trip. The Bruins' own doctor was to check me over, and we also hoped to see a couple of hockey games in the Boston Garden. We would stay at Eddie Johnston's home and help him celebrate his birthday. I really hoped I could make it, for this would be the first time since my injury that I'd see all my teammates together.

Chapter / 7

Ottawa looked wonderful to us. It was a clear, cold November day in this beautiful capital city of Canada, the kind of day that reminded me of our last week there, when Pat and I walked from the hospital to the park, idly enjoying ourselves just before I left the hospital. As we drove in from the airport, it seemed so good to be alive that I forgot for the moment my reason for going to Ottawa in the first place and for staying there as long as I had. For both of us, this was almost like coming back home.

Here was a city where I'd suffered the worst experience of my life, yet both Pat and I fell in love with the place. Part of the reason, of course, was that everyone had been so nice to us there, but I think it went deeper than that. Whether or not I nearly died there I'll never know, but I had thought I *might* die there, and so had Pat. When death seems that close, life seems even more precious. And, horrible as it all was, the weeks in the hospital welded Pat and me as close together as two people would ever be. Coming this near to a permanent separation had given us a greater appreciation for what we had and what we meant to each other. During the trip into town, I felt again the same warm wave of affection for her that had swept over me so often in the hospital.

Pat and I talked casually, neither of us expressing our true feelings, but the whole idea of being back in Ottawa for the first time since leaving the hospital made me particularly aware of her. I was glad she was there, glad she could share with me the surprising pleasure we found in being in this clean, bright, impressive city.

". . . I had somewhat the same thoughts," Pat said, "except that I couldn't forget the worst moments—the dread as Eddie Johnston drove Mary and me to the hospital the day after Teddy was hurt, the deep-rooted fears of permanent handicaps, the terror when Mike Richard phoned that Saturday morning after the hemorrhage, the despair when Teddy seemed to get worse, the complete crack-up when Dr. Ivan told Teddy's father he might have to be operated on again. These were moments that Ted never truly experienced because of his condition. To him, Ottawa was the place where he had recovered from what seemed the edge of death. To me, it was the place where he had been hurt and where he had then wavered for days between a normal future and one of dependency on others—or, perhaps, no future at all.

"Yet the city had wonderful memories for me, too. Throughout those weeks in Ottawa, we did solidify a relationship as rewarding as two people can ever hope to have with each other. Deep as our love had always been, Teddy had never been one to express it in so many words. He was a man, and in his mind men didn't get carried away by their emotions. Not until he was hurt did he find it possible to show his feelings openly. Now he doesn't try to hide them, which is good because it provides him with an emotional safety valve he never had before."

We checked into the Holiday Inn, the closest downtown hotel to the hospital, then walked over there. We saw Mama Schwartz and a few of the nurses we remembered, after which I began the round of routine examinations. I didn't see Mike Richard until he'd studied the results. He greeted me with a handshake and that quizzical smile that attracts everyone who meets him, and said, "You don't look like a guy who's been rapped on the head with anything."

I didn't feel like one, either, especially after Mike told me the tests showed a distinct improvement over the month before, when I had left for home. He added that if I continued to improve and really worked at it, perhaps I could fool everyone and make a hockey comeback.

That night we went out to dinner with the Richards and

the Demers. Afterwards, Guy Demers, who's an Ottawa businessman, said, "Come on over to our house. We've got something to show you." When we arrived, he led the way to a gigantic picture on the wall of his den. It showed a Montreal hockey player—John Ferguson, one of the toughest guys in the league, with whom I'd had several set-tos without always getting the best of it—with Bandaids all over his face, his stick in his hand, and his feet wide apart. Between his legs was the picture of me with the cat's face sticking out of my sling. The caption read: "Bug off, pussycat." Guy also read a bit of doggerel he had written, beginning: "I know a guy, Ted Green by name, who by the lumber did get tamed."

Of course, it amused us all—except for Pat. Any reference to the injury or its aftermath bothered her.

("It's foolish, of course," Pat said. "I know the boys rib each other over injuries, but it just doesn't seem that funny to me. I'm really not a killjoy. But every kidding reference to Ted's injury just rubs me the wrong way. He can laugh about it, and I'm glad he does because it relaxes him. I can't.")

As a matter of fact, that was the first time I ever saw Pat high. She never was much of a drinker, but Mike Richard persuaded her to down a couple of martinis, and that did it. She had made the trip to take care of me, but when we got back to the hotel that night I was taking care of her. She had a rough night and awoke with a stupendous hangover that didn't go away until we left for the airport.

Despite all the activity I felt fine, so we went on to Boston. Milt Schmidt and Eddie Johnston met us at Logan airport, and it was really great to see them and the old town again. Boston, of course, is our second home—or maybe our first now. We own a house in Lynnfield, where we spend much more time during the year than in our St. Boniface home.

Pat and I were staying at Eddie Johnston's in Stoneham, a suburb north of the city. Eddie had just married a terrific girl named Diane—I think he must have been the oldest surviving bachelor on the Bruins, since he was well into his thirties—and she and Pat became good friends almost on sight. But before going out to Eddie's, the Bruins wanted me to have a check-up with a Boston neurologist, Dr. Robert G. Ojemann, at the Massachusetts General Hospital, which is right near the Garden. Dr. Ojemann gave me an EEG, with much the same results as Mike Richard's. He, too, encouraged me to keep working; but I doubt if he thought I'd ever play again.

("I wasn't sure," Dr. Ojemann said. "If it had been anyone else, I'd have seen no chance at all, because Ted's left arm, and especially the fingers, didn't look very good. But Ted is Ted. There's nobody I've ever seen like him. He had terrific desire and determination, far beyond that of most people. He just refused to believe he was through, and I certainly didn't want to say anything discouraging. But from a medical and practical standpoint, it didn't seem promising. This was November 1969, about two months after he was hurt. If anybody had told me Ted would be on skates in a Bruins' uniform ten months later, I would have questioned his sanity.")

Later that day the Bruins held a press conference for me at the Garden. I knew all the Boston hockey writers, of course, and was glad to see them, as well as the sports people from other media. I didn't really want to go on the air, but couldn't avoid it. This was my first time since the injury, so I was a bit nervous, which made the left side of my face droop. As I began talking, I could feel my cheek and mouth pull together, but I still managed to get through it. I also answered questions and chatted with the press, all of whom were very considerate. I finally excused myself, and Pat, who had Eddie Johnston's car, drove me to his home.

We stayed with the Johnstons eight days, during which we had a wonderful time—saw a couple of hockey games and had great reunions with all the guys and their wives or girls. Pat stuck pretty close to me wherever we went. She was afraid I'd get overtired, and I guess she had a point.

We saw two games, but I just remember the first one. Pat sat with Diane Johnston up in the stands and I went to sit by the Bruins' bench. A few fans who saw me began applauding and calling my name. Word spread quickly through the Boston Garden, and soon everyone was standing to give me an ovation. I waved my good arm and tried to smile, but suddenly choked up and put my head down so no one would see the tears. Only when I sat down did the cheering stop, and only then did I regain my composure.

One night the whole team helped Johnston celebrate his birthday at a big party in Eddie's apartment. Everyone had champagne and we all had a wonderful time reminiscing, kidding around, and just enjoying ourselves. The guys really made fun of my speech that night. Except for Johnston, most of them hadn't heard me when it was real bad and they didn't realize how much I'd improved. It was still pretty bad by normal standards, and they called me Slushmouth and other names. I just stood there and grinned. All this is part of hockey because it keeps injured guys from feeling sorry for themselves. I never heard of anyone taking it seriously, and I certainly didn't. After all, these were the same guys who had attended a special Mass for me, had done everything they could to cheer me in the hospital, and had wept for me when things looked worst.

They kidded me about the way I let my arm hang loose, too. This was really good for me, because I forgot I had the damn thing most of the time. I'd stopped wearing the sling when I began doing little things with my arm, but most of the time I didn't think about it. This was one of the things I really had to train myself to do, and I had not been successful up to that time. When I walked, I swung my right arm naturally, but unless I thought about it, I just let the left one hang. Everybody constantly had to remind me. And it was months before I could swing it naturally. Until then, it was the same old story I'd first heard from Mrs. Platt, my therapist in Ottawa: *Make your dormant brain cells do the work of the damaged ones.* And, except when I was working with my left arm, the only way to do that was try to remember those messages of concentration: *Brain to arm—brain to arm—brain to arm.* I never thought of the kidding that way, but I realized later I could use it to remind me I had a left arm.

I didn't know until the next morning, when Pat woke up hung over, that she had once again become stoned on two drinks. And for the second time within a week! I don't believe she'd ever had two drinks in one evening before that trip, and I can't recall her drinking much since. Some people get the message quickly.

The party broke up around twelve-thirty when I suddenly felt terribly dopey and went into another room to lie down. The guys yelled goodnights to me, but I think by the time they left I was more asleep than awake. I saw them all once more at the other game we attended. A few days later we flew home to Winnipeg.

At that time—late November—I really began the job of trying to get into good physical shape. Besides the therapeutic exercises for my arm and fingers, I began working out not just to bring back my lost movements, but to harden myself up for what I hoped was my hockey future. Until that time, except for the Boston trip, I hadn't had much interest in hockey. My folks got the *Hockey News,* and I guess everyone in the family read it but me. When we were at the house they put on nationally-televised hockey games, but half the time I didn't even watch.

After the Boston trip my interest picked up a bit, largely because I had a sneaking little hope that maybe I could make it back for the following season—1970–71. That meant I would have to be ready to skate by September, when pre-season training began in London, Ontario.

I didn't talk much about it, not even to Pat. But she knew what I was aiming for—that's the way she is. She has an uncanny knack of reading my mind.

". . . It isn't a knack at all," Pat said. "I know my husband. Right from the start, even before we left the hospital, he was thinking of coming back for the opening of the 1970–71 season. It didn't take any great occult powers on my part to see that. Even when Mike Richard told him these things sometimes took a couple of years, Ted refused to believe him. Actually, I think Mike was trying to let him down easy. That was soon after Dr. Ivan had told Ted he didn't think the arm would come back at all, and Mike had talked about a 50-50 chance.

"Mike didn't think Ted would ever play again, which was why he said two years. That gave Ted plenty of time to get adjusted to the idea of forgetting hockey. Although Ted had those frequent spells of depression in the hospital when he told me he was afraid he'd never be right again, his real feeling was that when the next hockey season rolled around he'd be out there on the ice with the rest of the Bruins."

For the next month and a half I worked like hell. In December I joined the Business Men's Club at the Winnipeg YMCA, where my partner, George Hague, kept in shape, and I never missed a weekday. It was a mild winter for Winnipeg, which normally is pretty cold from November through February. The coldest day we had while I was going to the Y was around 35 below not counting the wind. That was pretty cold, but, even in my condition, I could go out in it. I'd been doing it all my life. And, as a matter of fact, 35 below in Winnipeg, where the air is clear and the humidity almost nonexistent, is more comfortable than Boston at zero.

The Y had a 90-yard track. My first day there I ran about 6 laps, something over a quarter of a mile, and gradually built that up to 15 laps, just under three-quarters of a mile. I started lifting light weights with my left arm, and got up almost to medium weights. I couldn't even manage one push-up the first time I tried, but by keeping at it I got myself up to six. I also did sit-ups and chin-ups.

I did this six days a week—not on Sundays—until about the third week in January. If George or one of my brothers couldn't pick me up, Pat drove me to the Y before ten in the morning. After workouts and a shower, I went home about noon, had lunch, and then slept for a few hours. I just loafed around the rest of the day, rarely leaving the house except for occasional dinner visits to my folks' house or Pat's. After supper I watched television (sometimes a hockey game, but not often), and was in bed by nine or ten, depending on how I felt.

Despite my improvement at the Y, I wasn't satisfied. I let my arm hang loose too much, and still had difficulty manipulating my hands and fingers. As the first weeks of January went by without much visible improvement, I suffered deep depressive periods. Around the middle of January, I was so low I refused to look at hockey on TV, read about it, or talk about it. I even tried not to think about it.

I started missing days at the Y, first one a week, then two, finally all six. Sometimes I sat in the living room chair, lifted my left arm as far as it would go (about halfway), and cursed at it. I talked to it, saying things like, "You sonofabitch, why don't you get better?" or "Here I work my tail off for you, and you don't even cooperate," or "Goddamit, if it weren't for you, I could play hockey right now." Then, disgusted, I would drop it into my lap and just sit staring into space, not thinking anything.

At other times, all my thoughts were negative. Instead of blaming my arm I blamed myself, thinking, *I'm crazy. I can't do it. Mike, Dr. Ivan, Mrs. Platt, everybody tells me I'm asking more of myself than any human being has a right to ask. I'll never play hockey again. Why don't I admit it and stop all this nonsense?*

Pat left me alone. She knew that only I could lick this

problem. She never asked why I stopped going to the Y, why I sat and stared, why I seemed to have lost my desire and determination, or what I was thinking. She didn't have to ask.

("I knew Teddy was going through a serious depression stage," Pat said. "I wanted terribly to help him, but there was nothing I could do. Any words of encouragement at that point would have sounded hollow and false. I just let him sit. He had had a rough time, and I saw no harm in his feeling sorry for himself for a little while. He certainly had a right to. He had fought this battle against huge odds, and had made amazing progress already. A bit of depression here or there wasn't going to stop him. He got himself into it and he'd get himself out, just as he had before. His brothers and parents agreed with me. There are times when you can help somebody in Ted's state of mind, and times when you can't. This was one of the times you couldn't, and we didn't try.")

Once in a while, somebody would stop by and take me for a ride. Whoever it was—Tony, Kenny, George, my dad —just passed the time of day. They talked about the weather, the Bruins, the old days when I was growing up in St. Boniface, friends—anything except my complete surrender to discouragement.

Whether I retrogressed or not is hard to say. I think if the depression had lasted longer I would have. But I was in pretty sound shape, and the few weeks' layoff wasn't long enough to make an appreciable change. Though my arm and hand didn't get better, they didn't get worse either. Once in a while I would move them. But no change.

One day Mike Richard phoned to invite us to a February dinner in Ottawa for the benefit of a boys' group. He also told me that near the end of the month I was scheduled for the last operation to put the covering on my skull. We accepted the dinner invitation, and looked forward to the change of scenery. Not until the day we flew to Ottawa did we learn that Wayne Maki would also be there for his trial before an Ottawa judge for assault with intent to injure. I wasn't particularly eager to see Maki, but my feelings weren't strong enough to call off the trip, because we didn't want to hurt Mike.

He met us at the airport and took us to the Skyliner Hotel, where the banquet was being held. (The Bruins had stayed there the night I was hurt.) That afternoon we read in the papers that Maki had been acquitted and would be at the banquet. At the time, I think somebody asked whether I'd pose for pictures with him. I didn't want to be contrary, but I had to refuse. It would be hard enough just to see the guy, let alone having my picture taken with him. I just said I didn't want to talk about him, and Pat steered me away.

When Maki arrived, he came over to where I was sitting. After we shook hands and mumbled greetings, he went to another part of the room. Later, I saw him talking for several minutes with Pat, but I don't know what they said.

* * *

"... Maki apologized for not speaking to me when we had met by accident in the coffee shop of the Chateau," Pat said. "Then he told me how sorry he was about the incident and that he was glad to see how well Teddy was doing. Of course, the last time Maki had seen Teddy—at the Campbell hearing—he looked terrible. Now, although his left arm usually hung uselessly at his side, it wasn't in a sling, his face wasn't so badly twisted, his speech was better, and the ugly head wound was less conspicuous because more hair had grown over it. Maki also said something about his testimony at the Campbell hearing, but it didn't mean anything to me because I hadn't been in the room where it was held. All I remember thinking was that Maki apparently tried to make me understand why he said what he said. I only replied, 'Look, put it out of your mind. It's a part of our lives that Teddy and I would just like to forget. Right now we don't bear you any ill feelings.'

"I really felt badly for him. He was very nervous and seemed more upset about seeing us than we were about seeing him. He finally shook hands and walked away. Believe me, I'm no admirer of Wayne Maki, but I think it took some moral courage on his part to talk to me at all. Much later, I remembered the letter we had sent him, but I never thought to ask him if he had received it."

Before we left the room where the head table guests were gathered, a couple of writers again approached me to get me to talk to Maki and pose with him. They were so persistent I just had to say, "I don't want any part of this. I don't want any publicity. I shook Wayne Maki's hand when he offered it, but I don't see why that should be blasted all over the papers. I'm here to attend this boys' organization banquet, and that's all."

They left me alone then, and as far as I know didn't make a big deal over my meeting Maki. They couldn't quote me because I didn't say anything. Although my speech had improved, it still wasn't clear enough for me to speak at banquets. All I did was acknowledge my introduction and sit down.

After returning home I continued to mope around, feeling sorry for myself. But in the last few days before flying to Ottawa for my final head operation I felt a little better, and actually did a few simple exercises at home. There was a question whether Pat would go with me. Her mother was sick and she hated to leave all three children with my parents. Still, she didn't like my traveling alone or being alone in Ottawa if there were complications. Mike Richard finally convinced her this was not a serious procedure and, in view of Pat's mother's illness and my improvement, he advised her not to come.

I left Winnipeg in good spirits. This would be the last operation. And I was thinking positively again. When I came home this time, I'd resume my workouts. And when the Bruins reported for pre-season training in September,

I'd be with them. I was sure—surer than I'd ever been. Let the arm be as perverse, as stubborn, as slow to react as it wanted. Sooner or later, before September, I'd make it come around.

Chapter / 8

Inserting the plate in my head would be the last operation in connection with my injury. So when I arrived in Ottawa, I was buoyant and happy. This was not just another hospital trip, for after this was over I could really concentrate on getting in shape for hockey.

I arrived in Ottawa on a Tuesday and went directly from the airport to the hospital, where I was checked in and assigned to a room on the third floor. As far as I knew, I was to have tests that afternoon and be operated on Wednesday. However, after I'd changed into pajamas, nothing happened. I waited about an hour, then called a nurse and asked, "What's going on? If I'm supposed to have an operation tomorrow, shouldn't they be taking tests today? Will you check this out with Dr. Richard?"

Half an hour later she returned and said, "The operation has been postponed to Friday, and you'll have your checks Thursday."

"What happens in the meantime? Am I just supposed to sit around here?"

"That's right."

After she left I got dressed, packed my bag, and started out, heading for Montreal to attend a sports show. As I passed the nurses' station my nurse said, "Mr. Green, where are you going?"

"I'm leaving the hospital."

"You can't do that. You're already checked in."

"Just watch me," I said. I hadn't even broken stride.

Downstairs I phoned Mike and said, "I don't want to hang around here all week. Is it OK with you if I go to Montreal?"

"Sure," he answered. "Just get back Thursday morning."

When I returned on Thursday, Mike came into my room and explained what he was going to do by drawing diagrams of my skull and the new covering. He would first drill holes in the skull, then mold an acrylic covering for the opening there. Although it was pretty difficult to believe the operation was all that easy, Mike didn't seem to take it too seriously. Before he was through, he had me convinced that this was no worse than treating a common cold.

"... Actually," Dr. Richard said, "it really wasn't a great deal more serious than I made it appear to Ted. But head surgery always entails some risk, especially when you work close to the brain. I wanted Ted thoroughly relaxed, my normal procedure with any patient, for with luck and no unexpected complications, this would be the last operation I'd have to do on Ted resulting from his injury.

"In these procedures, one is always tempted to insert the covering at the time of the original injury. That would be fine if you could be sure the patient would have no aftereffects. But to play safe I prefer to wait, and in Ted's case that was the proper thing to do. If he had hemorrhaged with the brain covered, the effects of the second operation would have been far more severe than they were. Just the time it would take to get the covering off might have been disastrous. As it was, with the wound still open, I could go right in there and operate quickly, easing the brain pressure with as little delay as possible.

"Some doctors use steel plates to cover open skull wounds, but I prefer acrylic. It's pliable, easy to mold, easy to connect with the skull itself. And, once hardened, it actually gives as much, if not more, protection than the skull itself. More important than anything, perhaps, is the fact that you can X-ray through it, which you can't with steel.

"Acrylic is a form of plastic. It is made of powder and liquid, almost in liquid form when you start working on it. You mix it like a cake batter and it immediately begins to solidify, although it remains pliable enough to manipulate throughout the operation.

"That begins by opening the scalp and baring the bony defect at the point of the injury," Dr. Richard went on.

"The brain stays closed—you're working only on the skull, which is covered by the scalp. The bony defect is directly beneath the skull, in which you have already drilled holes to take the acrylic when you're ready to insert it.

"When you have bared the bony defect, you put the acrylic, now mixed and starting to harden, over the hole, shaping it to the defect with your fingers. You trim away the edges like trimming away rough edges of still soft cement. Once it's trimmed to fit the defect, you fashion holes around the edges to correspond with the holes you have already drilled in the skull. You fit it over the skull and wire the two together, then put the scalp back over and secure it. This is basically the operation.

"By the time the scalp is closed, the acrylic has already begun to harden and become a part of the skull. It would take a terribly hard blow to break it again—at least as hard as the one Ted took originally. I don't think a glancing blow would break it any more than a glancing blow would cause a skull fracture.

"This use of acrylic instead of steel is a personal preference. Acrylic is just as strong as steel when it hardens. Some doctors even add a wire grid, but I think acrylic alone is protection enough. As time goes on, there's always a little overlap of the acrylic to the skull, but it's so slight you wouldn't know it was there unless you felt for it."

I went home a week after the operation, determined to be ready when the Bruins reported for pre-season training at London, Ontario, the following September, seven months away. Hockey has been my life for so many years that I could never be happy without it. I've played ever since I was a kid—not only hockey, but other sports as well. But hockey has always been my best game, and my heroes were all hockey stars. Even Mother became a fan, if only to understand Tony, Kenny, and me at the dinner table.

Unlike my brothers, who were born in St. Boniface, I arrived in Ericksdale, Manitoba, about 100 miles north of Winnipeg, where my father had a farm. The family happened to be there about the time I was expected. Dad had farmed up there before he came to St. Boniface to work for the railroad. The nearest hospital was 14 miles away. Ericksdale, which today has a population of 300 and was even smaller then, is still almost exclusively farm territory. My father hitched up a cutter (a snow sleigh) pulled by one horse, which he drove so hard the horse was frothing at the mouth when they arrived at the hospital. And I was born only a few minutes after they got there. The nurses were mad as hell at my father because once he got Mother to the hospital he was more worried about the horse than about her. The date was March 23, 1940, which up in that part of the world is still the dead of winter, even if the calendar does say spring.

As little kids, my brothers and I were crazy about sports. Although hockey came first, we played baseball and football, too. Tony and I were always together, always doing the same thing. Kenny's polio kept him from keeping up with us, but he played baseball and hockey anyway. According to Dad, Tony and I were about equal skaters, but I was more aggressive. I don't think I ever considered pro hockey as a career because I didn't think I had a chance to make it, and my father didn't push me. There were a couple of boys around St. Boniface whose dads made their lives miserable, always on them to practice so they could grow up to be NHL hockey players. Neither made it, mostly, I think, because by the time their dads were through with them they hated hockey. My brothers and I played because we loved it. And though Dad is proud of me now, when I was young he never mentioned my playing pro hockey.

All over Canada there are classified leagues for youngsters, beginning at about age seven. The kids start in Playground hockey, then, depending on their age and ability, move up in order to Bantam B, Bantam A, Midget, Juvenile, Junior, and finally Professional. Actually, most boys who end up as pros have to make it first in Juniors, although more and more are coming out of college into either minor- or major-league hockey. Ken Dryden, the big goalie who starred at Cornell University and later attended McGill Law School, is typical of the new-breed NHL star. He'd had less than one season in the minors before the Canadiens brought him up just in time to star in the 1971 Stanley Cup playoffs, which Montreal won. When I was growing up, Junior teams were sponsored by NHL clubs, and every member of a Junior team belonged to the sponsoring big-league club. Today, some Junior teams are sponsored, but the players aren't committed to the sponsoring team because at age 20 they go into a draft pool and are subject to the luck of the draw. The only draft we had when I was a kid was from one NHL club to another.

Tony and I played together all the way up to Junior hockey. We wanted to stay together, but I was picked up by the St. Boniface Canadiens and Tony by the Winnipeg Rangers. Even though both were amateur clubs, this automatically committed me to Montreal and Tony to New York if we were to turn pro. It was only then I definitely decided to try and make it to the NHL.

My strongest asset was my aggressiveness, a characteristic Tony didn't have. He loved hockey as much as I did, but he either couldn't or wouldn't take it as seriously. When I played for St. Boniface, I knew I'd never settle for anything less than the NHL, which at that time meant the Canadiens. Tony simply didn't care that much. He wanted to enjoy hockey, and he played just for the hell of it. But I had to charge, hit, and get into every scrap available. That was my style then, and it continued to be my style right through my early days with the Bruins. This combativeness won me the nickname "Terrible Teddy Green," which I now frankly resent. Any aggressive hockey player is likely to get into fights. True, I looked for them in those early years, but after about 1965 I never went out of my way to find them. I didn't have to. They came to me. But the nickname stuck right up until my head injury. I never minded being the league's tough guy, but I took exception to my reputation as a guy with a perpetual chip on his shoulder. I wasn't mad at anybody. As a defenseman I had a job to do, and that was my way of doing it.

I went into Junior A hockey a year ahead of Tony, who was still playing Junior B. By then Kenny was in Bantam A, making Sunday a pretty busy day for my parents. Often they went to a Bantam A game in the morning to watch Kenny, a Junior B game in the afternoon to watch Tony, and a Junior A game in the evening to watch me. Later that year Tony went into Junior A hockey. The only year we actually opposed each other was my second in Juniors, when Tony played for Winnipeg, which was in the same league as St. Boniface.

That year Mother sat with the St. Boniface fans and Dad with the Winnipeg fans whenever the teams opposed each other. I guess if my parents had their choice, all our games would have ended in a tie, although life was easier for them when St. Boniface won, because I came home happy and Tony not too terribly disappointed. When Winnipeg beat us, I was upset and hard to live with. I hated to lose.

Although Juniors range in age from 16 to 20, I started playing for St. Boniface at 15½, when I was a sophomore at Holy Cross School. Because there were hockey classifications for practically all ages, the high schools didn't have hockey teams. The good players were all in one league or another. I was a tough, hard-nosed kid, and really deserved the nickname "Terrible Teddy" then. Always in fights, always bashing the nearest someone with something—stick, elbows, or bare hands—I think I put in more penalty time than anyone in the league. One year I was suspended for 12 games of the 32 in the regular Junior schedule. I hadn't yet learned that you don't do your team any good sitting in the penalty box. For years, both in Junior and NHL hockey, I averaged at least one penalty a game. I didn't get smart until after the 1964–65 season, when I spent 156 minutes in the penalty box during the 70-game season. Since then I have calmed down considerably.

In 1958 St. Boniface lost to the Winnipeg Braves in the Manitoba Junior playoffs, and the Braves picked me as a replacement for the Canadian Junior playoffs, the winners of which are Dominion Junior champions and recipients of the Memorial Cup. This sort of replacement is normal procedure all over Canada. The winning team in various parts of the Dominion has the option of adding players from other clubs in its section, since the team represents the whole province.

By then, my third year in Juniors, I already had the reputation for being a tough kid who never missed a fight and spent too much time in the penalty box. I still hadn't earned a dime from hockey, although I would have in my last year if I could have stayed out of trouble. I don't remember exactly how many penalty minutes I was allowed, but St. Boniface promised me some money if I could keep away from the penalty box for X number of games. Even with that incentive, I couldn't collect.

I psyched myself up for the Dominion playoffs by determining to keep my head and try to behave. By then I was practically my present size—five feet, ten inches, and 200 pounds. I had a real good playoff series, took only a reasonable amount of penalties, and helped the Winnipeg Braves win the Memorial Cup in the finals against the Peterborough Petes.

The Memorial Cup series was always well scouted by the six NHL teams (it still is by all 14 clubs today), and the Canadiens brought me to pre-season training because of my play for the Braves. This, of course, gave me a tremendous thrill. Although we lived nearer Toronto than Montreal, the Canadiens were the glamour team and the Montreal Forum the glamour arena. The club trained in the Forum, where it drew capacity crowds even for exhibition games.

At 18, I was the youngest player in camp. And during that one training season with the Canadiens I had a curious distinction which I doubt anyone shares. I think I'm the only guy who's dumped all three members of the Richard family in one game. Maurice (the Rocket) was nearing the end of his sensational 18-year career. Henri (Pocket Rocket) was in his prime, well on his way to a long career that hasn't ended yet. And Claude (Vest Pocket Rocket) never made it in the NHL. But that fall they were all on the same line in pre-season training. The squad was divided into four teams, which played each other in exhibition games as bloody as any regular-season contest. In one of those battles I knocked off Maurice, Henri, and Claude Richard in succession when they came down my side of the ice.

I was disappointed when the Canadiens failed to keep me, for I thought I'd done pretty well. Still, I was the last man on the squad to be sent down before regular-season play began. Of course I had a hell of a lot to learn, but few 18-year-olds know that. I ended up with the Winnipeg Warriors in the Western Hockey League. The club was owned outright by a guy named Jack Perrin, though I played as the property of the Canadiens my first year there.

At the end of the 1959–60 season the Canadiens protected me in the pro draft until the very last minute, when I guess there was somebody else they were more anxious to keep, and they took me off the protected list. Lynn Patrick, then general manager of the Bruins, had personally scouted me, and on his recommendation Boston drafted me for $20,000.

The following season—1960–61—I was all over the place: Kingston of the Eastern Professional Hockey League, a Bruins' farm club; back in Winnipeg, this time as Bruins' property; and, for a very short time, Boston. I played in only one game there, and managed to pick up a penalty during the few minutes I was on the ice. It was the first of many in Boston. At Winnipeg, where I had put in 109 penalty minutes in 70 games the year before, I piled up 127 minutes in 57 games. I either started or got into almost every fight on the ice, and probably collected more major penalties than anyone else in the league.

Curiously, I played in Winnipeg either with or against two of the very few professionals who died on the ice, Bill Masterson and Wayne Larkin. Both came from Winnipeg and were good friends of mine. Masterson died during a regular NHL season game in January 1968. (He's the only player ever to lose his life in an NHL game.) He hit his head on the ice while playing for the Minnesota North two of the very few professionals who died on the ice, Stars. Larkin, who died at age 28, had a heart ailment and didn't know it. During preseason training with the New York Rangers a few years ago, he skated up and down the ice once and just dropped dead. And I was almost number three on that fatal Winnipeg list.

The Bruins were in deep trouble, a fifth-place team needing help almost everywhere, when they bought me from the Canadiens. They were last in 1960–61, for the first of five straight years, and they went eight seasons without making the playoffs. Lynn Patrick, one of the nicest guys I know, later told me my aggressiveness had caught his eye, and he felt that even if I didn't score much (I never do) I could make waves with the Bruins. I guess he was right. I played for them through those bad years, and though we weren't going anywhere, I kept fighting.

Actually, the "Terrible Teddy" reputation was built up

over those four years, from the 1961–62 season through the 1964–65 season. As a Boston regular I amassed over 100 penalty minutes each year, and even increased that number as I went along. The first season I spent 116 minutes in 66 games in the penalty box. The next three years, playing 70 games each year, I had, in order, 117 minutes, 145 minutes, and 156 minutes.

I was proud of that record then, but I can't say I'm particularly proud of it now. It's pretty stupid to get banished by the referee for breaking rules, although sometimes you can't help it. In any contact game, you'll break some rule, intentionally or otherwise, but hockey is so fast you'll often get away with it. I think I picked up a good deal of penalty time because of my reputation. Since the officials watched me closely, they naturally caught me more often.

After I smartened up, I still couldn't keep out of the penalty box. In the 1967–68 season, my first full year after being out most of two seasons with knee troubles, I collected 133 penalty minutes in 72 games. Personally, I don't think that's so awfully bad. Two two-minute penalties a game is 144 minutes in a 72-game schedule, and plenty of guys pick up a pair of two-minute penalties in one game.

My knee woes, which spread out over two seasons (1965–67) necessitated four operations. The difficulties began when my right knee popped after hitting Eric Nesterenko of Chicago in Boston in 1966. At the end of the season the Bruins sent me to the Mayo Clinic in Rochester, Minnesota, for knee surgery.

Mayo doctors operated on my right knee late in April, and I didn't get out of there until June. My leg was in a cast during July and I was confined to crutches the next month, yet I reported to the Bruins for pre-season training on schedule—September 10. After a week in camp, Hap Emms, who was then the Bruins' general manager, and a man I disliked intensely (I was not alone), called me into his office in London, Ontario, and said, "Ted, we don't think you're skating as well as you can."

I stared at him. "You can't be serious! Don't you know I've spent the whole summer in hospital beds, in a cast or on crutches? I'm only off the crutches a few weeks. Of course I'm not skating as well as I normally do. I'm skating on one leg and turning in one direction. If I had any brains I wouldn't be here at all, but I thought I could help the team."

Emms didn't even apologize—in fact, I don't believe he said anything. Though he never again criticized my skating.

Still favoring my right leg, I started the 1966–67 season, and played in 13 games before a virus infection knocked me out of hockey for five weeks. I went along pretty well after my return, but played only 14 more games before my left knee popped when I grabbed Guy Talbot in a game against Montreal at Boston. I limped off the ice and went to the Newton-Wellesley Hospital. (The Bruins have since switched to the Massachusetts General.) The doctor couldn't find anything wrong because by then the cartilage wasn't caught but was floating around somewhere in my knee. Then the knee hemorrhaged and the doctor drained it and put a cast on it.

At home that night I went nuts from the pain. Back at the hospital the next morning, they found my leg had swelled inside the cast and an infection had set in. They drained my knee a second time and then decided to operate to get the floating cartilage out. Less than a week after I got home, the knee started swelling again. Back at the hospital I got a shot of cortisone, some more draining, and assurance everything would be fine. After this happened twice more in the next few days, I got permission from the Bruins to go home—I didn't tell them why.

The reason for the trip was to see an orthopedic specialist in Winnipeg, Dr. Dan Bigelow, who was a good friend of mine. After examining the knee, his eyes popped.

"By God, Teddy," he said, "I think you've got a hernia of the knee. That's the first time I ever saw one."

To make sure, he called in several other doctors and had a dozen or so pictures taken, which confirmed his diagnosis. He told me the sooner I had surgery the better. But first I had to get back to Boston for permission to have the job done in St. Boniface and also to pack up the family—Pat, Karen, and Chris—and move them all home.

In Boston I went to see Weston Adams, Sr., owner of the Bruins. (He is now chairman of the board, and his son, Weston, Jr., is president.) After I told Mr. Adams the whole story and said I didn't want to go back to the Newton-Wellesley Hospital, he asked me to see the doctor there once more, and if I wasn't satisfied I could have the job done in St. Boniface.

I saw the doctor in the Bruins' aid room, and he gave me the same old song—he'd drain my knee in the morning and then it should be OK. I thanked him, got dressed, and walked out. After calling Mr. Adams and getting his permission to go home, I packed up the family and we left.

Incidentally, I might explain why I went directly to Mr. Adams, something I normally wouldn't have done and wouldn't do now. All this business should have been handled by the general manager, but that was Hap Emms, and I wasn't about to go to him for anything. Mr. Adams had always been very nice to me—as he is today—and I felt I could talk with him. Now, with Milt Schmidt the G.M., I wouldn't bother the Adamses. Milt is one of nature's noblemen. I'd talk anything over with him.

Back in St. Boniface I entered the hospital in April for two operations. All the time I was having trouble with the left knee, the right was developing a bone spur, which Dr. Bigelow thought should be removed.

My right knee was OK in a couple of weeks, but my left was painful for so long I cursed that Newton-Wellesley hospital doctor every day for two months.

After another rough summer, I managed to report to training camp in better shape than the previous year. This time I didn't have to worry about Emms because Schmidt had replaced him and Harry Sinden, with whom I had once played at Kingston, was now the coach. I then had two good years in a row, making the NHL all-star team in the 1968-69 season. That was the year before Wayne Maki's stick landed on my head.

So you can see I was a pretty experienced hospital veteran by the time I landed at Ottawa General that September night in 1969. And now, back from the last operation on my head, I was ready to start seriously my return to hockey. But there was a difference. Before, all I had to worry about were my knees.

Chapter / 9

I don't remember asking Pat Mascarin to marry me, and I don't remember her saying she would. Neither of us recall exactly when and how we met, nor just when we fell in love, nor how we knew it was love. I was quiet, almost sullen, not easy to like let alone love. I didn't feel the way I acted. I just was shy, suspicious of strangers, slow to make friends.

People who first meet us wonder how Pat and I ever got together in the first place. I was an athlete, with few interests outside of sports. Pat, who had graduated high school and worked in the credit department of a Winnipeg retail store called the Hudson Bay Company, was interested in art and music. She knew nothing about sports. I doubt if she could tell a hockey stick from a baseball bat.

Even before I was hurt, I spoke too fast, slurred my words, and wasn't easy to understand. I graduated high school, too, but you'd never know it by the way I talk. Pat's voice is soft, her grammar excellent, her manner gentle. My voice is hoarse, my grammar questionable, my manner curt.

Yet we're perfectly matched, and in the years since our marriage in April 1963, we've developed a depth of feeling almost beyond love. We understand each other. We accept each other as we are. Neither of us changed after we were married. We never had to.

Professional athletes are among the most self-indulgent —not selfish, but self-indulgent—people in the world. In a way, they have no choice. They make their living from their bodies, which are specially trained for the particular sport they play. When your body is your bread and butter, you take extra precautions to keep it in condition. Everything you do is geared to the effect it will have on your body—the mechanism that makes you click.

This can be tough on wives. And some find it difficult to cater to men the way athletes expect wives to cater to them. The only way women can accept the situation is to adjust themselves to their husband's foibles. I guess everyone has little foibles. Professional athletes have big ones. They must eat certain foods at certain times. They must sleep certain hours. They must not be upset by domestic problems, particularly on the day of a game. Some of us are impossible after losing a game. I try not to be, but I can't help it. If we lose, I blame myself or say nothing.

Pat never changes. She talks when she knows I want

her to talk. She's quiet when she knows I want her to be. She knows instinctively just how to handle me. Yes, I have to be handled. I'm quite aware of that. So, thank heavens, is Pat.

I play hockey, love hockey, build my life around hockey. But when I lay in that Ottawa General Hospital, especially after the hemorrhage, and prayed to live, it was for Pat and the kids, not for hockey. Yet once I was on the road to recovery, once I realized there was a chance I might play hockey again, my love for the game rose right back to the surface, and everything I did was geared for hockey. I wasn't about to die any more. My problem was to make a hockey comeback. That didn't mean I loved Pat any less. It only meant that I couldn't spend as much time with her now.

"... I don't think Teddy and I ever formally met," Pat said. "We just sort of grew together from being neighbors, after I started working. My family moved from another section of St. Boniface to Dubuc Street. Teddy lived on Youville, the next street parallel to Dubuc, and our back yards faced each other. Except to say hello as neighbors, we didn't pay much attention to one another at first. It wasn't until 1961, the summer my sister got married, that we began showing any real interest in each other. Our parents were friends—they still live in the same houses in the Norwood section today. Teddy and I kept meeting in the yard, and he would sometimes help me wash my car.

We started dating in August, but that didn't last long because he had to report to the Bruins for pre-season training. That 1961–62 season was his first full year with them.

"We carried on sort of a desultory correspondence which didn't mean much because I was still dating other boys and I suppose Teddy had his own girl friends around Boston. It really wasn't until the next season that we became serious. We didn't decide to get married in the sense that he proposed and I accepted—we just sort of took it for granted. In February 1963 I visited Boston. And it was then we made our wedding plans. We were married April 27, 1963, after Teddy came home to Winnipeg following the end of the Bruins' hockey season.

"Of course I was a hockey fan by then, although I didn't know much about the game. I had seen Teddy play for the Winnipeg Warriors, but never with the Bruins. I was sort of shocked to learn he was supposed to be the tough guy of the National Hockey League, and at first I couldn't understand it. He may have been a terror on the ice, but he was a lamb off it—a sweet, considerate guy who acted as if he wouldn't swat a fly."

Pat didn't like my reputation any more than I did. I remember once early in our marriage she asked me why I played so hard.

"Look," I told her, "they expect this of me right now. This is the only way I'm going to stay up. If I don't knock people down, which is what the fans expect me to do, I don't keep my job. I'm learning. The more I learn, the more they'll depend on my ability instead of my roughness. Right now I'm the team policeman. If somebody gets hit, it's up to me to go after the guy. This helps attract attention to the Bruins, because we're not winning."

Once you acquire a reputation in any professional sport you seldom lose it. Even Boston fans didn't notice my change after I came back from my knee injuries. One reason was the nature of the team, which instead of being simply a few good players, was rapidly developing into the unit that won the Stanley Cup in 1970. By the end of the 1968–69 season I was an altogether different hockey player from the "Terrible Teddy Green" of old. I got into fights—yes—but I didn't look for them. I played defense as it should be played, which meant controlling the puck, making plays, rushing the puck out of our zone. My own teammates knew I was playing a different and more effective game, and so did the officials.

This was what I had to build back up to when I got home from Ottawa after the last operation. But in order to do it I needed full mobility just to skate well enough to help the team. And, although I didn't have to go looking for fights, I had to get back my nerve to do the defense job I was supposed to do. That meant hitting guys coming at me, and wading in to help teammates in trouble. Being home with a new plate in my head was a step in the right direction, but I had a lot of ground to cover to get back to where I was before my injury. That's why the fight with Dan Maloney of Chicago in December 1970 was to be so important to me.

During the two months immediately after the plate was inserted, I worked harder and harder. I had gadgets of all types in the cellar: pulleys, bars, that sort of thing. I continued to work out at the Y, and I began taking long walks. Eventually, I rode a bicycle about four miles a day. All this kept me away from home more and more, but if I were to rebuild my body, it had to be done. There was no other way.

My physical condition improved, but not fast enough. I still didn't use my left arm much. Time and again I caught myself letting it hang as I walked, doing things with my right hand that I should have been practicing with my left, favoring my left side. No matter how hard I tried, I couldn't button my own shirt with my left hand; it was too numb. And I'll always have trouble with buttons.

There were things I wanted to do—indeed, had to do if I was to be ready for hockey by September—that I couldn't manage. Because I could not lift my left arm high enough, hunting and golf were out. Although I wasn't fearful of my skating, I knew I was far from ready to manipulate a hockey stick. I never worried about skating—only about my arm movements. The legs were fine. My speech was improving. I could do certain exercises with my left arm, but not enough.

As the weeks went on, my interest in hockey became sharper, and this time I retained it. Led by Bobby Orr and

Phil Esposito, the Bruins were the class of the league, and even when they failed to win their division championship, they were hot favorites to win the Stanley Cup. When the playoffs neared, I became more and more excited. Even a slight scare at home didn't calm me down.

One day in the basement, where I had gone for my daily workout with the equipment there, I bent down to get something, straightened up fast, and whacked my head on one of the joists. It wasn't just a tap, but a real belt, hard enough to make me see stars. My first reaction was fright. Then, when I realized nothing had happened, I just sat there and laughed. I thought it was pretty funny.

("I didn't," Pat said. "I was scared to death. But since it struck Teddy as funny, I laughed with him. This is one of the odd things about hockey players. They're so used to laughing at the injuries of others they seem tickled pink when they get hurt themselves. It's the nature of the beast, I suppose.")

The Stanley Cup playoffs began on April 8, 1970. Boston won games one and two of the first round on home ice, lost the next two in New York, then swept games five and six to get into the semifinals. We were to meet Chicago in this series, and the victorious team was almost certain to win the cup, since the other semifinalists, the Blues and Penguins, were expansion teams. St. Louis had always been best among the first six expansion clubs, but they still weren't in a class with the six original NHL clubs. St.

Louis won their series with Pittsburgh, while we swept Chicago in four straight to go into the finals.

The importance and the pressure of the playoffs had no effect on the calls I got from teammates. Bobby Orr, Eddie Johnston, or Turk Sanderson had been phoning all year at least once a week to see how I was getting along. Sometimes they called alone, sometimes with other guys who got on the phone to call me "Dum-Dum" or "Slushmouth." We were always kidding and laughing about things that struck us funny, including the effects of my injury. I loved every minute of it, even when they'd call collect as a gag. Besides cheering me up, those calls really touched me. It was good to know that even in the thick of things they hadn't forgotten me. And when they continued to phone after the playoffs started, I got a special thrill.

One of them—I think it was Bobby—thought I should come to Boston for the playoff finals. The Bruins' front office would pay my expenses, but I didn't know whether I wanted to go or not. At first I told myself the excitement would be too much for me, but I knew that wasn't the real reason. I just didn't feel I deserved to be there. I had contributed nothing to the club's success, and I didn't want to do anything to call attention to myself. But the boys began insisting and Pat wanted me to go, so at the last minute I decided to do so.

All the way to Boston, I continued to have ambivalent feelings. I wanted to be there, yet didn't see what I could add. The closer I came to the city the more doubts I had, and when the plane landed I nearly took the next flight back to Winnipeg. The Bruins had already won the first two games of the finals in St. Louis, giving them a chance to clinch the cup at home. Everyone from the front office to the gallery gods wanted this to happen. And it never occurred to me the Bruins wouldn't sweep all four games after they'd won the first two in St. Louis.

As soon as I arrived in Boston, I got caught up in all the Stanley Cup excitement. That the Bruins were not only in the finals but in a key position to win, hit me as the plane landed. Somebody picked me up at the airport—I think it was Frank Caruso, a friend of mine—and we joined Bobby Orr at a restaurant for dinner.

It was there I first realized that because of the paralysis in my left hand I couldn't sign my name. Since my head injury I'd signed it only once—on the three-year contract the Bruins sent me. That time, holding my left hand with my right, I traced my name, a slow, painful operation. I held the pen between my first and second fingers and pushed it with my right hand. I suppose someone could have signed for me, but I wanted to do it myself. When I finished, my left arm throbbed from the effort, and the result looked no more like my signature than this craggy face of mine looks like Pat's.

I had no other occasion to sign my name until the night I went to dinner with Bobby Orr and Frank Caruso. A fan recognized Bobby and came over for his autograph, which he courteously gave. (Bobby is more than just a close personal friend, he's one of the nicest guys I've ever known. He has a strong sense of obligation to his public. As a superstar, he is bothered more often for his autograph than anyone in hockey, and, to the best of my knowledge, he's never refused except when in a hurry. And then he apologizes.)

This time, the person who approached him recognized me and asked for my autograph also. Before I could say anything, Bobby told the fan, "Teddy's left hand is still paralyzed and he can't sign." The fan understood.

Before I left Boston, however, I ran into a most unpleasant situation on this same issue. I was having a drink at Caruso's place, the Diplomat, when a youngish woman asked me for my autograph.

"I'm sorry," I said, "but I can't sign my name."

She gave me a withering look, as if to say, "What's the matter? Are you too big a shot to give an autograph?" and walked away in a huff.

I felt awful—so bad I wanted to go over and explain the situation, then decided to wait until her party got up to leave. I could tell them when they passed my table, which they would have to do to leave the place. When the people approached after finishing dinner, I stood up and said to the woman who had asked for my autograph, "Excuse me, ma'am, but I'd like to explain——"

Before I could say more, an older woman with her spoke in a voice that carried across the room. "Athletes like you have a hell of a nerve refusing to give autographs. Who do you think you are anyway?"

I turned away and didn't give her a chance to say more. Perhaps she wasn't a real hockey fan. If she had been, I'm sure she would have known about my left side. Perhaps there was no way of her knowing I was left-handed.

That was the most unpleasant incident, but not the only one. Time and again after I rejoined the club, I had to refuse to sign: "I'm sorry, but I'm left-handed and I don't have full use of my hand yet."

Once a guy said, "Use your right hand."

"Are you right-handed?" I asked.

"Yes."

"Can you sign your name with your left?"

The guy shook his head, grinned, and apologized.

By putting pressure on my fingers, I later was able to sign. But it was always an ordeal. For months my signature never looked the same twice. Today, however, it's coming back, and I'm pretty good with autographs. At least they now look like a reasonable facsimile of my original handwriting.

Thursday, May 7, was the night of the third game of the Stanley Cup finals, the first in Boston. Before the game I went into the locker room, where I found everyone loose and relaxed. I didn't think going in there would affect me, but when I saw all those pals of mine confidently looking forward to winning the cup I'd fruitlessly helped chase for nine years, a lump came into my throat.

Nine years is a long time, and most of them had been rough years for all of us. Only a comparatively few who had been with the Bruins since 1957 were in the locker room that night—Johnny Bucyk, the dean; Eddie Westfall, who had broken in with me; and Eddie Johnston, a year behind me. The rest hadn't been through the ordeal of finishing fifth and sixth year after year.

Instead of one captain the Bruins had four assistant captains, with Bucyk the senior man because he'd been with the club the longest. The others were Westfall, Esposito, and me, although I didn't count myself. I felt wistfully out of it. It wasn't easy for me to realize that I had nothing to do with this victory coming up. I hadn't played a minute of regular-season hockey all year. This cup victory would be won without my lifting a finger.

As I sat on a trunk, the guys came over to assure me I was part of this club, as much a part as if I'd been playing right along. But I didn't *feel* part of it. I thought of baseball's Tony Conigliaro, knocked out of action for the 1967 season when he was hit in the face by a pitched ball. The Boston Red Sox won the pennant in one of the closest races of major-league baseball history, clinching it on the last day of the season. Conigliaro must have felt just as I did when he sat in the Red Sox locker room on the day they clinched. Maybe I felt even more useless. At least

Conigliaro had played half a season and done his part to win plenty of games. I hadn't done anything.

When the boys left the locker room for the start of the game, my spine tingled as John Kiley, the organist, played the team song, "Paree," and the packed house of 14,835 rose and roared. I went to the bench as unobtrusively as I could and sat alongside it. By then the crowd had quieted down, and I thought I would go unnoticed. They never announced I was there, but a few nearby fans recognized me and started yelling my name. The next thing I knew, the whole crowd was back on its feet, cheering and clapping for me. With my eyes filled and a lump in my throat, I finally stood up and waved, then sat down again.

This was no ordinary game. It was for the Stanley Cup. Every goal we scored brought the cup nearer, and when we won 4–1, putting us only one game short of a sweep, I was as excited as the fans.

The fourth game, May 10, was tied 3–3 at the end of the regulation three periods. I remember saying to Coach Harry Sinden, "Wouldn't it be great to win the Stanley Cup in overtime?" Then, just before we went out for the beginning of that, I added, "It would be even better if Bobby scored the winning goal."

And that's just what happened. Only 40 seconds after the opening whistle, Orr got the winning goal, and the place went mad. I can remember feeling great as I stood beside the glass that protects the crowd from flying pucks. I was excited for Bobby, for the team, for Sinden, for the crowd. Excited for everyone. And then I started to choke up again. Sinden and the players all jumped the boards, and somebody began rolling a rug out to center ice for the presentation of the cup.

Suddenly, happy as I was, I felt I had no business being so close to the ice at that moment. As I pulled back from the glass, I saw Sinden talking to Bucyk, Esposito, and Westfall, and the next thing I knew Bucyk and Esposito, one on each side, had me out on the ice with the rest of the team.

That time I really did blubber over. The tears were rolling down my cheeks as I thought, *Here's Harry Sinden's greatest moment in hockey, and right in the middle of it his first thought is for me.* Because of Harry, there I stood hugging one guy after another. When Bobby Orr hugged me we were in tears. All the emotions came together—my injury, my missing out on such a beautiful year, the memories of all those bad years I had lived through with the team, and the knowledge that when this finally happened, everyone wanted me to enjoy it, too. Glad as I was to be there, however, all I could think was, *How can you feel a part of something that you haven't given anything to?*

Johnny Bucyk skated around the rink holding the Stanley Cup high so everyone in that berserk crowd could see it. And there it was. There was the trophy that meant the in 29 years. The fun would come later. But that trip around the ice by Johnny had an unforgettable emotional impact on us all.

Back in the dressing room, I stood aside and watched pure bedlam take over. Once again I felt detached from this wonderful group of guys who had won hockey's most coveted prize—but without me. I went over near the entrance to the showers, where I stood on a box and watched the boys howling and slapping and pouring beer and champagne all over each other. I stood there 10 minutes or so while the guys celebrated. Finally I went over to the aid room, still enjoying everything but thinking this was their party, not mine. I felt a little like an intruder.

Just then Phil Esposito, sopping wet and smelling like a wine cellar, popped his head in and said, "Green, you've got two minutes to take your clothes off. Otherwise, we'll drown you the way you are."

The next thing I knew he was back with three others, all armed with open champagne bottles and beer cans. As they dragged me into the crowd of yelling hockey players, they squirted me, clothes and all. Pretty soon I was laughing and screaming, drenched from head to foot. They led me to the Stanley Cup and made me put my arms around it and hug it, just as each of them had done. Soon I was as crazy as they were, grabbing champagne bottles and beer cans, squirting the stuff everywhere. It was the only time that whole year I really felt a part of the hockey club, and I was glad I had come to Boston.

The next morning I went back to the Garden, the starting point for a Stanley Cup parade given the team by the city of Boston. My intention was to see the guys for the last time and say good-bye before returning to Winnipeg. I went to the parking lot behind the Garden, where they were assembling.

Bucyk, Esposito, and Westfall were already in the lead car with the Stanley Cup. When Harry Sinden saw me, he came over and said, "Ted, you get into that car, too. You're an assistant captain, just like the others." It was the second time within 12 hours that Sinden had included me just as if I had played all year. And I'll never forget him for that.

The others welcomed me, and we started driving toward the street, where crowds were already gathered. Once there, a policeman on a motorcycle moved in behind us. As the parade progressed and no other motorcycle police were in evidence, I decided perhaps this one was there to guard the Stanley Cup, but I was wrong. Eddie Johnston told me later he asked the guy to follow just in case something happened to me.

A thoughtful gesture by a wonderful guy.

Chapter / 10

Before leaving Boston for home, I made arrangements to work out during the summer with Gene Berde, who runs a health club at the Colonial Inn in Lynnfield. Berde, a tiny man with bright blue eyes and a heavy accent, won everlasting fame among Boston's baseball fans when he trained Carl Yastrzemski of the Red Sox in the winter between the 1966 and 1967 seasons. By the time the 1967 season began, Yastrzemski was in excellent shape, and he had the best year of his professional life. From then on, Berde trained a lot of pro athletes. And he agreed to train me, starting July 1.

I had one more trip to make before returning to Boston. My court trial in Ottawa, which had been postponed several times, came up about 10 days after I got home from the Stanley Cup playoffs. I don't know what caused the delays, but I wanted the thing over with just as quickly as possible. The judge who had acquitted Maki, and therefore could not have sat in judgment of me anyway, died shortly after Maki's trial. Maki had been tried for assault with intent to cause injury, the original charge against me. After Maki's acquittal, they knocked my charge down to common assault. Much less serious. Every so often I got some official-looking notice, but no summons until late May. I don't know today, and even Clarence Campbell doesn't, precisely who brought the charges. Officially it was the Crown, but everyone in Ottawa who might have done it has denied doing so—the chief of police, the Crown Attorney, the few other officials in a position to make charges. In fact, it was grossly discriminatory, since no fans were involved—only Maki and me—and neither of us had brought charges against the other.

I went to Ottawa alone for the trial. The judge and the court officials were all very nice. I had no trouble. Edward Houston, the Ottawa attorney the Bruins had engaged for me, took over my defense. Depositions were read, witnesses were called, and it was all over in two days. I was completely acquitted.

While in Ottawa I saw Mike Richard, who gave me an EEG. He found things improved, but warned I still might have a convulsion.

"If one starts, but doesn't get full-scale, forget it," he said. "That's an abortive [incomplete] convulsion. But if you have a real one, I want to know about it."

This scared me a little, until Mike told me an abortive convulsion meant nothing, and it was unlikely I'd have anything worse.

("When anything threatens Teddy, his mind works overtime," Pat said. "While he was in Ottawa that last trip, Mike Richard had said something about possible deterioration if he had a full-blown convulsion, although this is very rare. Teddy was frightened to death about deterioration. After all his work and planning, any backsliding would have been tragic. His arm was pretty good by then, and his fingers were starting to come back. I still didn't think he'd be ready for hockey, because it was now only three months before he was due to report to London, Ontario, for the Bruins' pre-season training. This didn't bother me at all. I was hardly enthusiastic about his returning to a business that had nearly killed him. On the other hand, since it was what Teddy wanted, I wanted it, too. My only real worry was this convulsion business, and what it might do to him.")

I did have a couple of abortive seizures. Both came in June, after the trial. The first was shortly after my arrival home. Everything was fine, then suddenly the left side of my face went numb one day. It started high and worked down until my upper lip drooped over the bottom one. At the same time, my fingers got tingly, as on the night I was hurt, then became numb. It's hard to describe; except for this sudden numbness, nothing else seemed to happen. My left arm and left leg weren't affected at all. I just stood there, before I sank down on the couch, thinking, *Oh, my God, is it starting all over again?* I was alone in the house, and wondered just how far this thing would go. Mike had said it could be anything from a glassy stare to an actual fit, with me shaking on the floor.

I was on the couch for less than five minutes when everything began coming back. The fingers were the first to feel normal. The left side of my face began straightening out. I spoke aloud, and it came out right. Gingerly I got to my feet, and by then I felt OK again.

When I told Pat about it, she said, "It sounds abortive."

"I'm sure it was," I answered. So we decided not to call Mike.

I forget where I was the second time it happened, but that, too, was just an incomplete convulsion, which spread no further than my fingers and which I came out of within a few minutes. Once again Pat and I decided not to call Mike. In fact, he didn't find out about them until the following September, when I saw him in Ottawa. He assured me it wasn't anything to worry about, and just to keep on with the dilantin. I've been taking three pills a day since getting out of the hospital, and will continue to do so indefinitely, possibly for the rest of my life.

I continued my own regimen of special exercises, trying to get the lingering numbness out of my fingers and become able to raise my left arm. This had been a problem from the start, and I hoped Gene Berde, who had a million gadgets in his small gym at the Colonial Inn, would help me with it.

Both Tony and Kenny had been after me to start playing golf again. One May day Tony said, "Come on, Teddy, it's time to go out and try your golf."

"I don't have the strength, coordination, or muscle control in my left arm to swing a golf club," I said. "And how the hell can I grip one with so little feeling in my fingers?"

"You'll never know until you try," he replied.

Playing golf with my brothers was a dream I'd had in the hospital. And here they were ready to go. I'd been putting off golf because I was afraid of looking bad. I love the game, had shot in the mid-seventies and low eighties, and occasionally got down to par.

When we reached the first tee I said, "I'm not going to keep score."

"We'll do that."

"I don't want anybody doing it," I said. "I know I'll be bad so my score won't be anything to remember."

"You've got to know what you score," Kenny said. "Otherwise you'll never know when you improve."

I finally gave in, and stepped up to the first tee, a par four hole requiring a good drive for position to reach the green with an iron. When I took a few practice swings, I found it impossible. I couldn't grip the club with my left hand, and my left arm didn't have the necessary coordination for a decent backswing.

If I had been with anyone except my brothers, I think

I'd have quit right there. But they kept encouraging me, and telling me I couldn't hope to get my golf game back if I didn't start playing. I teed up the ball, took my stance, and tried a few more practice swings. I finally brought the club around awkwardly but hit the ball fairly well. Maybe it went 150 yards—in the fairway—but I had a pretty long shot for the green.

I hate to hear about golf games stroke by stroke, and I'm certainly not going to do that now. All I can say is that my putting was better than I'd expected, and the rest of my game worse than I'd feared. You can't score when you can't swing, and my swing was gone. I finished with a 105.

But I realized Tony and Kenny were right. I couldn't improve unless I played, so I began playing regularly, sometimes with them, or with George Hague, or with casual friends. By the time we left Winnipeg for Boston, where I'd start working out with Gene Berde, I was shooting in the nineties and my swing had improved. Golf was good for me. My two biggest problems were coordination of my arm and controlling my fingers, and swinging the club required me to do both.

Late in June the whole family flew to Boston. Friends had rented a house for us and we planned to move immediately. But when we saw the house needed plenty of work before we could comfortably move in and was short on furniture, I said, "Pat, I don't like this place."

"Neither do I," she agreed.

"OK," I said. "Let's stay at the Colonial until we find something."

A few days later we got together with Ken Hodge and Johnny McKenzie, teammates who both owned homes in Lynnfield. After talking things over with them, we decided to buy ourselves a house, preferably in Lynnfield. Through an agent we found something we liked, although it wasn't available until September 1. We then advertised in the Boston papers. While we were trying to decide what to do, we had a call from a man named Eric Johnson, whom I'd never met. He was spending the summer in New Hampshire and had a house in Danvers, right near Lynnfield.

"The place is empty," he said. "If you'd like it, it's available. The only trouble is, we'll be back right after Labor Day."

"Great," I said. "We just bought a house we can't get into until that time."

Eric, who has since become a good friend, owned a house so completely furnished we didn't even have to buy towels. And when he came home we moved into our own place, where we now live year round except for about two months.

My work with Gene Berde began on schedule. You haven't lived until this little 65-year-old wonder gets his hands on you. A former coach of the Hungarian Olympic boxing team, Gene teaches by example, and how the hell he does it at his age I'll never know.

This man, who once told Yastrzemski he wouldn't even be a third-class athlete in Hungary, was slightly easier on me. But I'm sure it was only because of my partial paralysis. He started me on simple breathing exercises—at least, they were simple for him. Like most people, I breathed with my mouth instead of my lungs. Learning to breathe properly sounds a good deal easier than it is. But once you've mastered it you've increased your endurance 100 percent. And these exercises can be done anywhere. They require nothing but your own efforts. Although Gene worked with me only in the mornings, he had me practice breathing all day.

Next came calisthenics, with breaks for deep breathing at the end of each exercise. After 10 minutes I was exhausted, while Berde, who did everything I did, was fresh and sharp. Then he made me jump rope, an elementary enough exercise for any little girl from five years on. Except it nearly killed me after about half a minute. Gene then took a rope and skipped for three minutes without even working up a sweat.

I began slowly on his special gadgets because he knew it would take me more time than most to work into a groove of strenuous exercise. He had me running on a treadmill, operating wall pulleys, riding a stationary bicycle, doing deep knee bends, push-ups, high kicks, chin-ups, arm stretching, tossing the medicine ball, forward and backward somersaults, 60-yard sprints, and working on a devilish contraption called the Swedish wall ladder. It's a heavy, multiple rope ladder forming a vertical and horizontal grid. You scramble up it like a monkey—or at least Berde does—and every muscle of your body is exercised.

Because of my condition, I couldn't do many of these things at the start, but Gene had me doing them all before summer's end. He also encouraged me to play golf to build my fingers and left arm movements. And he talked to me endlessly about my physical condition, telling me I could do anything I'd done before, and just as well.

This I found hard to believe. Hockey, being primarily a contact sport, requires absolute confidence. Berde kept after me all summer, and well into the hockey season, to forget my injury and hit guys the way I always had. He assured me I was just as strong as I'd ever been, though at first I could not believe him.

In addition to breathing exercises, he had me do other things at home, because, as he said, "An hour with me is nothing. I can't build up your body. All I can do is show you how."

When I wasn't working with Gene, I was at the beach or on outings with the family. And I played golf at the Colonial. As the summer wore on, and I progressed physically under Berde's supervision, my golf improved tremendously. Before the summer was over I was in the low eighties. A real milestone.

". . . Ted Green was one of the most dedicated men I've ever handled," Berde said. "When I first talked to him I said I could help him only if he cooperated completely with me. I've worked with disabled people, but never with a handicapped athlete trying to make a professional comeback. I am not a bashful man. I think I can do anything, just as I try to teach my clients to think. But Green was a special case.

"When he came to me, he'd obviously done a lot of work himself. I doubt if anyone with such serious brain damage barely nine months before would have been in as good shape as Green. One of the things I liked most about him was his determination to make it back to the Bruins. Without this spirit, I don't think he could possibly have reported for pre-season training by September.

"I really don't know how much I did for him. I showed him the exercises. But he did the rest. And whatever success he later enjoyed came through his own efforts.

"There's no way I can compare Ted Green to any other professional athlete I've ever handled. For courage and determination, he was in a class by himself."

Pre-season training was scheduled for September 11 at London, Ontario. We had a new coach, Tom Johnson, who had been a special assistant to Milt Schmidt and sort of a superscout for the Bruins. Boston gave him the coaching job when Harry Sinden shocked us all by resigning a day or so after we clinched the Stanley Cup.

Tom and I had known each other for years, and were defense partners on the Bruins before his serious leg injuries had knocked him out of hockey for good. Although this was his first coaching job, he knew us all, knew hockey, had been around the NHL for over 15 years. We had confidence in him.

I went to London not knowing if I could play hockey again or not. I hadn't been on skates since the night I was hurt. But skating would be no problem. I wasn't concerned about picking that up right away. After all, few NHL players skate between seasons. In that respect we were all starting from scratch. And except for such fine movements as picking out coins by feel or signing my name, I could do everything I had always been able to do with the fingers of my left hand.

My biggest job now was mental. And even as I reported to Johnson for the opening of the training season, two things worried me. One was the helmet, the first of several I tried as the season progressed. I had never worn one playing hockey before because, unlike now, when helmets are required in Juniors, they hadn't been in my time. The helmet was a damn nuisance. I hated wearing it. However, I would adjust to it because I had no choice. I certainly couldn't risk another head injury.

But from the day I arrived in London until well into the 1970–71 season, I had a far more serious problem to lick than the helmet. For the first time in my life, I was afraid. All the assurances from Mike Richard, Gene Berde, and Pat couldn't straighten me out. The left side of my body had been severely injured, and now I was gun-shy. I had to learn all over again how to use it in a hockey game.

And that, although I didn't realize it at the time training started, would be the most difficult hurdle of all.

Chapter / 11

When I kissed Pat and the kids good-bye and headed for London, Ontario, and pre-season training in September 1970, I was on edge. Saying I would again play NHL hockey and the prospect of actually doing so were two different things. Ordinarily, except for my rookie season, training meant nothing. It was just a period to get in skating condition, and veterans like me took it for granted.

Hockey pre-season training is shorter than in any other major professional sport. Baseball and basketball teams spend about six weeks. Pro football takes up most of the summer. But hockey lasts less than a month. We showed up at London about September 13 and the season was scheduled to start October 9.

Everyone tried too hard to make me feel at home—as if this were just another camp. I had seen these guys several times since my injury, but always under social rather than hockey conditions. Even when they (I try to say "we," but it never seems to come out that way) won the Stanley Cup, the boys had done everything possible to make me feel a part of this championship team, a full member in good standing. But only for those few ecstatic moments in the locker room had I felt I really belonged.

But now in London, where it should have been different, I'm not sure it really was. Every man in the Bruins' party, from Milt Schmidt and Tom Johnson down, wondered what I could do. When I went out on the ice, it was my first time on skates since the injury. And the boys were watching me. I could almost feel every eye in camp on me.

Can he come back? Can he skate? Can he handle a stick? Can he do the job? Can he ever be what he was before? Can he help us—really help us? I knew that was what they were really thinking. And some, I'm sure, were looking at me from a strictly practical standpoint: *We did it without him before. We want him to make it back for his own sake. But if he doesn't, will it make any difference?*

Obviously, no matter how good a team is, there's always room for improvement. The Teddy Green of 1968–69 would have made the great 1969–70 team still greater. This didn't matter because we won the Stanley Cup.

But what could the Teddy Green of 1970–71 do? The first question was my skating, and as it turned out, that hadn't suffered at all. Professional hockey players must be great skaters, not just good ones. Fans are apt to forget that. They're so accustomed to the skating they take it for granted. But the first prerequisite for major-league hockey success is skating. You must be able to move fast in any direction and be able to change direction in a fraction of a second. You must stop on a dime and start at the same instant. You must bounce off an opponent, the boards, or up from the ice faster than in any other sport. If you can't skate outstandingly well, you can't hope to be a pro hockey player.

I passed that test easily. In less than a week everyone in camp knew my injury had not affected my skating. I could handle myself as well as ever—in fact, better than some of the guys because I was in better shape. Actually, I reported in the best shape of my career. Gene Berde's regimen had made me hard as nails.

But I had been very apprehensive about my skating. Except for the week in camp before I was hurt, I hadn't skated in 17 months. On the night before practice began, I got Frosty Foristall to open the rink so I could sneak in a session alone. After half an hour of skating I was surprised how good it felt and how well I did. That was what made the first week so easy. And I was with my old teammates again, who'd helped me over those first early hurdles.

The opening exhibition game was something else. When the Chicago Black Hawks came to London, Ontario, to play us, things were tougher than I had expected. I trembled when I first went out on the ice, and continued to do so all through the game. They scored a goal on each of my five shifts. Naturally this bothered me, although I managed to laugh about it later.

It wasn't so funny when we went to Kitchener to play the Rangers. That time I trembled in the locker room, and I couldn't stop when I went out on the ice. After my first shift, during which I felt completely disoriented, I left the ice thinking I'd rather be somewhere else.

During the one-hour bus ride back to London, I sat alone and thought of what had happened. More than anything else, I worried about being scared on the ice. It wasn't getting hurt that worried me, but not performing properly as a hockey player. I had no confidence, no puck control, no real passing ability.

This was my problem in training camp, and it would remain my problem well into the season. I couldn't hide it, and didn't try. I'm sure everyone on the club saw I had a long way to go before I could really help. For me to play on this Stanley Cup championship team would at first help me far more than it would the club. My job was to turn that around. Somewhere along the line, Tom Johnson would have me in there because there was nobody better available at the moment. And somewhere along the line, Johnson would use me because he needed me, not because I needed the work.

It was a dilemma for everyone. Believe me, no man ever had more help from more people. Everyone wanted me to come back. Everyone wanted to help me. Everyone admired me for trying. I appreciated all this. But more than anything else, I had to be needed.

It's pretty hard to be needed on a club like the Bruins. This team had so much talent, was so powerful offensively and defensively, had so many fast, young, brilliant players—with more waiting in the wings—that one man more or less made little difference. Perhaps I should say one man like me. A Bobby Orr or a Phil Esposito, both superstars, would certainly be missed.

Before I got hurt I was a good defenseman, a hell of a good defenseman, alternating with Bobby Orr at right defense. Every team needs five regular defensemen—two sets to spell each other and a spare if somebody gets hurt. Orr, of course, is in a class by himself because, even on defense, he is an offensive threat. I'm not so presumptuous as to compare myself to him. But before I was hurt I never weakened the team when I was out on the ice, and defensively I believe I strengthened it.

Since I usually played with the penalty killers or the power players (the five skaters on the ice when the opposing club is short), I was often on with Bobby, particularly when we were shorthanded. I had been on the all-star team and was considered among the top three or four defensemen in the league.

All this was behind me. I knew that. I wasn't going to make this 1970–71 club on the strength of what I had done before. Having won the Stanley Cup without me, they could afford to go along without me again—in fact, I'm sure they were planning to. Nobody thought I'd be ready before January at the earliest.

The four regular defensemen the year I was out had been Orr, Ricky and Dallas Smith, and Don Awrey. The fifth man had been Gary Doak part of the time and Bill Speer the rest. Doak, a rookie, had been taken by Vancouver in the expansion draft. Speer, a rookie, had started the previous season at Salt Lake City, after the Bruins drafted him from Pittsburgh in the summer of 1969. Two other rookie defensemen, Bob Stewart and Ron Plumb, were in camp, but both had just come up from Canadian Junior hockey and probably did not fit in the Bruins' plans at such an early stage in their careers.

I really don't think the Bruins expected me to be anything but a spare defenseman when I first reported. The problem, however, was that I needed ice time. I couldn't improve sitting on the bench.

Tom Johnson knew this, let me set my own pace, and soon made it evident he would give me a break. I played in every exhibition game as Awrey's partner, just as I had before my injury. Don and I had been together so long we could practically anticipate each other's moves. In the course of my comeback—if it were to succeed—the heaviest burden would be on him. He would have to cover for me if I got confused or was not able to handle a situation. This was to happen frequently because my timing was way off and my confidence was gone in the early stages of the season.

* * *

". . . There was nobody in hockey I owed more to than Teddy Green," Awrey said. "I didn't make it permanently with the Bruins until the 1967–68 season, although I had played for them all season long two years before. In those days, Teddy was always picking me up, showing me by example what to do, talking to me in the locker room, on planes, in hotels. He gave me the valuable tips most hockey players have to find out for themselves. If I'm a good defenseman—and I'm not a bad one—it's because Teddy helped me. And now that he needed help, nothing would give me more pleasure than to give it to him. I knew he'd have difficulty readjusting, knew that he'd be in trouble, knew that it would take him a few months of championship hockey to get back in the groove. I was amazed that he could skate at all in training. But, being Teddy, I knew that nothing was going to stop him, and nothing did."

". . . After what Teddy had been through, I couldn't imagine his ever coming back," said Frosty Foristall. "But when he came to Boston to work with Berde during the summer, I felt quite differently. I saw him come back from those knee injuries, and they were tough enough. But now all I could think was, *My God, a year ago they were picking pieces of skull out of his brain*. If it had been anybody but Teddy, I wouldn't have believed my eyes. But that guy is the most determined athlete in the world. He has more willpower than anyone I ever knew."

". . . He was on the spot in training," said Phil Esposito. "We all wondered if he'd be able to skate, let alone play hockey. I remember asking him the first day, 'Did you skate yet?' and he didn't answer—I don't know why. All I know is that every single one of us was watching him while trying not to. We didn't want to embarrass him or make him feel we were putting him through some kind of test. We all felt the same way—if he could come back we'd be a stronger team, and we were already the best team in the league. And once I saw him skate, I knew he'd make it back."

". . . We were all pretty deeply moved when we saw him on skates in training camp," said Ed Westfall. "That was the first time I guess everyone thought, *Maybe he really will come back.* He had to learn so much all over again. All we needed was one look and we knew he'd have no trouble skating. He looked better on skates that first day than most of us, and he was in good shape. But right from the start, he made terrible demands on himself. Too many, in fact. This caused him to get down on himself, to blame himself for lost games, for goals scored against us when he was on the ice. Nobody should chew himself out for these things. We're a team. Where were the rest of the guys? Somebody made a mistake before the man with the puck ever reached Teddy. But no. All that went through his head was, *I blew it.* Any goal Teddy thought he blew, everybody on the ice blew—the man who lost the puck in the first place, the forwards for not back-checking fast enough, the goalie himself."

* * *

I fretted over a lot of things in those early days. My timing was terrible. I couldn't adjust to guys coming down on me with the puck. Before, I'd instinctively know whether to skate up and meet them or hang back and wait. Now I had to debate with myself, and by the time I'd made up my mind, the guy was past me and heading for the cage.

I fretted over the damn helmet. I would have given anything to get rid of it. But I knew that was out of the question.

I fretted over my inconsistency. I'd show a flash of form one moment and follow with a bloop. I'd make a good block of the puck and follow with a clean miss. I'd make an accurate pass and follow with a wild one. I'd control the puck one minute and lose it the next.

I had never realized how much there was to hockey. For eight years (the season I was out would have been my ninth and the new season my tenth), I had done everything automatically. Now I had to think first and then act. But in hockey there's no time for thinking. It's an instinctive game. And my instincts seemed to be dead.

I even fretted over my inability to keep going at top speed for any length of time. I thought it was due to my injury, which had caused fatigue all through my convalescence. But no hockey player can keep going indefinitely. The game is too fast. That's why it takes 16 skaters to do the work of five. (I'm not counting goalies, who have constant let-up periods when the puck is at the other end of the ice.) That's the reason most of those on the bench are regulars who will probably put in as much ice time as starters. Getting tired isn't due to old injuries. Hockey is a fast, tiring game. And you must have fresh players ready to go into action on a second's notice.

Yet, early in the season especially, I worried about getting tired. I did tire faster than I had before. The demands I made on my legs and my wind were terrific. I had to prove that I could keep going as long as anyone. I think in the later part of the season I could, but not at the start. I had to overcome both rustiness and fatigue. I could do it only by playing regular shifts, and, although I had minor disagreements with him later, I owe a lot to Tom Johnson for giving them to me. Early in the season, every time Awrey went out I went out. And I was the weak link in this tremendously strong team.

A defenseman is the last bastion on the team before the goalie. On a given night, Eddie Johnston and Gerry Cheevers seem able to stop anything. But every clean shot taken at the goalie is a potential goal. It's up to the defenseman to keep opposing puck carriers from getting those clean shots. Of course, some shots can't be stopped by a goalie, no matter how hot he is. And if he's having a rough night, a good many he might otherwise stop slip by him.

For a defenseman to lose the puck after he has control of it is inexcusable. And I kept losing it all the time, something I'd never done, even in my rookie days. A great defenseman like Bobby Orr moved the puck with great ease, carried it down himself, or teamed up with someone else to get it down. A good defenseman will also carry the puck out alone or with another man, but not as often or as effectively as Orr. Well, I couldn't carry the puck down at all. Often, I'd simply end up behind my own net, holding the puck and waiting for Awrey or a forward to come by and pick it up from me.

I couldn't "deke" guys the way I used to. "Deking" is faking an opponent to get around him with the puck. It takes fast reflexes and clever stick handling—faster reflexes and far better stick handling than I had in those early games. I couldn't block shots as I had before—absolutely essential for a defenseman. When the puck is coming your way you've got to block it to gain control of it and to keep it from getting behind you and threatening your goalie.

Another difficult thing to relearn was to keep my head up, particularly at our end of the ice. When you carry the puck around behind the net, you must control it by feel with your head up, so you can look down the ice and see how the play is forming, where the opposition is, which teammate is free, which direction you should go. This rule applies to all puck carriers, for when you carry the puck in on an attack maneuver, you have to know what the opposing defense is doing, which way to move if you've got a potential shot on goal, where your men are, and how well they're being checked by the opposition. You can glance down at the puck occasionally, but not for long. The game is too fast. A man can come out of nowhere and steal it from you or check you heavily into the boards—which often happened to me—if you don't keep your head up.

This last business bugged me badly. I'd never had trouble doing it before. Why now? God knows I tried. I gave myself pep talks right on the ice: *Keep your head up. Know what's going on. Carry the puck by feel. You always could. Shape up!*

For a while I blamed the helmet, but I knew it wasn't that. Nor was it the long layoff. I just wasn't yet able to play hockey at the NHL level. And my only solution was to learn and learn and learn again.

I was like a golf duffer taking lessons from a pro. *Keep your head down. Keep your eye on the ball. Keep one elbow and the opposite knee stiff. Don't try to kill the ball. Watch your arms. Watch your wrists. Watch your grip. Follow through. Don't look up—don't look up—don't look up. You take care of your swing. The ball will take care of itself.*

It was the same in hockey. Elementary rules I had always followed weren't elementary anymore. I had to think of them. And I would never be the old Teddy Green until I could follow them without thinking.

If you grow up with a sport you develop this instinctiveness as you go along, just as you develop instinctiveness in everything else you do. You learn right from wrong, the simple courtesies, proper table manners, respect for others, and the hundred other lessons of a child growing up. They become ingrained. Whatever the reason, my hockey instincts were gone. And now I had to get them back.

I fretted because all my game was at our end of the ice. It was as if I couldn't venture beyond my own blue line on my own initiative. True, I moved up with Don Awrey when we had the puck at the other end because I had to guard the right side of the blue line to keep the puck in if it were shot my way. But even that I did with reservations. Sometimes I stood there praying the puck wouldn't come in my direction, for fear I would miss it or mishandle it.

Any hockey fan knows that the defenseman must get the puck in, preferably by shooting at the goal, as soon as he gets his stick on it in an attacking situation. Before I was hurt, I had a good shot and could slap or wrist the puck in hard. Now, when it came to me, I looked for a teammate to pass it to. I had no faith in my shot, no faith in my ability to shoot it fast and hard the 60 feet from the blue line to the net. I was in trouble—deep trouble—in those early games.

Chapter / 12

For me, the 1970–71 hockey season was made up of peaks and valleys. There were times I felt like the Teddy Green of old, when I knew I was helping the team, when I did the right things at the right time, often without thinking about it. The less thinking I did, the better I played. Obviously, I was at my worst the first couple of months, but then I began to see improvement. By late February or early March I was about 90 percent of the way along the comeback trail.

There were thrills and disappointments. The worst, of course, was the loss of the Stanley Cup. We were knocked out of it in the first round in a seven-game playoff with the Canadiens, who eventually won it all. The star of our series—and those that followed—was their young goalie, Ken Dryden, who made fantastic stops against us and everyone else the Canadiens had to play on their way to the championship.

But without taking anything away from Dryden, few of us were really "up" for the playoffs. We all made mistakes, once blowing a 5–0 lead, and certainly didn't deserve to win. We all suffered a letdown after clinching the Prince of Wales Cup for leading the league in the regular season. Possibly we were fat cats, and certainly the Canadiens were hungry. Even so, we forced an inspired Montreal club, with a goalie who seemed all arms and legs, to seven games.

I believe I had a fairly good playoff. I played a strong defensive game—strong enough to make me feel I should have had more ice time than I got. That I stayed out of fights, I think, hurt me as far as my critics were concerned. What they forget is that fights don't make good defensemen, a lesson I learned years ago. My job is to protect my zone and my goalie, and I did that successfully most of the time I was on the ice.

Defensemen are frequently never noticed unless something goes wrong. Their mistakes are then obvious because the direct result can be disastrous to the team. I made mistakes, certainly, but I did the right thing far more often than the wrong.

I don't know where people got the idea that Tom Johnson benched me in the fourth game for poor play and kept me out most of the seventh game for the same reason. What really happened was that, as the playoffs progressed, he seemed to have less and less confidence in me. I had trouble understanding this because in the first few months of the season when he didn't have confidence in me, and I didn't have confidence in myself either, Tom felt the loss of a game was less important than building my confidence. And, by using me as much as he did, he helped me develop my confidence. I owe a great deal to Tom Johnson. He let me relearn hockey the only way I could—by playing me regularly and showing me he felt I could do the job I eventually did.

I don't know what his thinking was during the playoffs, but I do know I was a damn good defenseman by then—not as good as before my head injury, but almost. Maybe Tom didn't agree. But whatever his reason, my long sessions on the bench at a time I knew I was playing well just bugged the hell out of me.

". . . I never lost confidence in Ted," Johnson said. "But it sometimes seemed he thought he could do more than he could. It had nothing to do with confidence, but with his own health. Here was a man who had made a miraculous comeback through terribly hard work, really grim determination, and great dedication. In the early part of the season, I used him for his own sake. He could never come back if he didn't play. I wanted him on the ice as much as possible, but I had to watch him. He showed flashes of form, but tired visibly as games progressed in the first few months of the season. I wanted him playing and healthy, and I don't think it would have helped him to leave him in during the late stages of close games.

"Whenever a goal was scored against us while he was on the ice he blamed himself, particularly in October, November, and December. We lost a game in Detroit which he persisted in saying was entirely his fault—that he had made key mistakes which cost us at least a tie. Mistakes happen in every game, and everybody makes them. Ted was always too quick to blame himself."

In mid-season Johnson said, "Let's stop being Green-watchers. Every time he's on the ice everyone glues his eyes on the man. Teddy Green does not need and shouldn't have to be given any more special treatment than anyone else on the club. He makes mistakes, but he made mistakes before he was hurt. When he does something good, people cheer him to the rafters; when he does something bad, everyone bleeds for him. Green wants to be just another hockey player, and he's improving all the time. He doesn't want to be an object of pity and he doesn't want the hockey world thinking he's a superman. All he wants is to be treated like everyone else."

In the fourth playoff game, at Montreal, after playing only five minutes in 1½ periods (the same thing happened to Awrey), I finally blew my stack. All the rest of the time Bobby Orr and Dallas Smith were on the ice. This made no sense to me at all. Between the power play, penalty killing when we were short a man, and playing defense about three times as long as usual, Orr was being asked to do more than was reasonably possible even for a superstar of his magnitude. By playing Awrey and me more, Johnson would have given Orr some badly needed rest.

I'm not trying to be noble about this. At the time I squawked, I wasn't thinking of Orr but of Teddy Green. And when I lost my temper on the bench, I yelled invective at Johnson, using some pretty strong language and pulling no verbal punches. He didn't bench me for poor play. He benched me for the things I said and the way I said them, and I'd have done the same if I'd been in his place.

At least Tom held no grudge because he let me play my regular turns in the next two games, but he benched me again in the final stages of the seventh game. And I kicked to him that time, too. Except I was more careful with my language. His answer, I thought, was a mysterious one. All he said was, "Teddy, I didn't bench you for poor play, but because I had to make a change."

My old enemy, the helmet, helped me in the third game when I was accidentally hit on the head by Frank Mahovlich of the Canadiens. He had just lost the puck, and as he passed me his stick hit me on the forehead, which was protected by the helmet. However, the blow, with the hardest part of the stick where the shaft meets the blade, also cut across my right eye and caused a deep gash on my nose. Mahovlich didn't even know he'd hit me. The whack sent me to my knees and stunned me for a few seconds. My eyebrow and nose were bleeding pretty badly, so I had to skate to the bench.

Tom Johnson came right over and asked if I was OK, and I said, "Fine." I guess maybe he didn't believe me because I heard him tell Ricky Smith, "You're up next, Ricky."

"Like hell he is," I said. "I'm going out."

We had a few words—I don't recall what, but it was more a spat than an argument—and Ricky turned to me and said, "Teddy, maybe I'd better go out there."

"I don't care what happens," I said. "I'm going out."

When the next shift came, I jumped over the boards and went on ice, and continued to play my shift for the rest of the game. My nose bled off and on for about three days, but the only stitch I took was in the eyebrow. I was damn glad I had the helmet on.

This was the second helmet I wore during the season. The first was too tight. The one I used later was much more comfortable. It had an air cushion going all around my head and was much lighter than the early one. But even that was hardly a substitute for no helmet at all. I had thoughts of going out there without one a good many times during the season, and I still think about it.

After the playoffs, Johnson said, "I didn't treat Teddy any differently from anyone else. The closer you come to playoff climaxes, the more important every move you make. I saw we were in danger of losing the series to Montreal, and I did what any coach would do—juggled men around, made changes, tried constantly to find the right combination. Teddy resented that I didn't use him more, and I can't say I blame him. But I didn't use Awrey much more than I used Green. I was trying to put together a winner, and I couldn't think of any single individual—only the team as a team. I wouldn't have done it differently before Ted was hurt. I did what I felt I had to do to beat a great club."

Looking back on my comeback season, I can see a lot of improvements and a lot of faults. There's no question I lost that game in Detroit. I was completely disoriented out there. I tripped over my own feet, fell without even being hit, and gave the puck away I don't know how many times. Two or three of those mistakes resulted in goals for the Wings—goals that cost us the game.

Everyone who saw the game could see how badly I played. I just put together a lousy game. I wouldn't have minded criticism because I knew I deserved it. I hadn't yet developed my instincts or recovered my timing, but even that was no excuse.

I remember one game—I'm not sure which team we were playing—when I made an inexcusable blunder. I blocked the puck, had complete control of it, and should have flicked it into a corner out of danger. Instead, I hesitated a second, which gave the man who had brought the puck in the time he needed to chip-poke it through my legs and into the cage. That was something I had never done before because my reactions were so much quicker.

And it's something that now I've a season under my belt, I don't ever expect to do again.

The early part of November was especially bad for me. I made so many mistakes in the first period that Tom simply had to bench me if the game was close. I didn't mind —in fact, I was grateful to him for putting up with me as much as he had. Playing so badly made me withdraw into myself more than ever. I just couldn't socialize with the other guys. If I couldn't contribute something good, I couldn't feel part of the team.

Mad at myself, I sulked, discouraged people who tried to talk to me, and often lost my temper. One instance that stands out in my mind was a game against Toronto at Boston late in November. I spent the whole day psyching myself up for it—just concentrated on the game from the time I got up in the morning until the game got under way. I really wanted to play my best, and I hoped this method would work. But I was uptight when the game started, and when you're uptight you handle the puck like a hot potato. The first shift I made a bad pass which landed right on Norm Ullman's stick. He had a clean shot at the goal but hit the post and didn't score. But the mistake was there for everyone to see, and when my turn was up Johnson benched me.

Having spent the whole day getting ready for this game, I was really mad—mad at myself and mad at Tommy. I was like a kid when he sent someone else out. I threw down my gloves and stick and helmet and started mumbling. Somebody—I think it was Turk Sanderson—tried to calm me down and even picked up my stuff. By then Ricky and Awrey were already on the ice and I threw the helmet again, except this time it landed on the ice. I remember thinking, *The hell with it. I'm not going out there to pick it up.* Then, as Ricky and Don came in while Orr and Dallas Smith went out to relieve them, Tommy said, "Get ready, Ted. You're going out next shift." From then on I played good hockey all through the game, trying harder and concentrating more than I had all season. If Tommy benched me as a strategic move to get me to play better, it worked.

I think my first real good game was against the Canadiens in Montreal about a week later. That was the first time I really got involved in the game, maneuvering the puck well out of our own zone and making good plays. One reason for this was that Orr couldn't play because of an injury and I knew Tom Johnson was depending on me. Afterwards, Johnson congratulated me. I felt particularly good because Mike and Margaret Richard were at the game. Even though they rooted for the Canadiens, it was wonderful to see them—the first time in a couple of months. We had a chance to talk briefly after the game. They recognized I had done a good job.

Then we came back home to play Pittsburgh, a much weaker team than Montreal, and I was awful. The first time I went out there, I had the jitters. As I stood at my right defense spot, I felt my knees shaking. I couldn't figure out why I should be so nervous after such a good game in Montreal. But it was the sort of thing that kept happening to me all through that part of the season.

". . . At first I just dreaded going to games because I felt so uncomfortable for Teddy," Pat said. "I felt I was him on the ice. He was trying so hard to do everything, and yet I could tell he wasn't doing what he wanted. He was disappointed in his play and there was no way he could get going. He couldn't handle the puck. He had trouble seeing—you know, you need eyes in the back of your head when you play pro hockey. It's something that's just instinctive, and he'd lost that completely.

"Some games I could tell after the second period that he was becoming involved. He'd start playing the way he had before he was hurt, but he had to work himself into it. Sometimes, it would take him almost until the end of the game to get with it. He'd be just raring to go when the game was all over. Then on the way home afterwards, he'd say, 'Pat, I'm playing like a rookie.'

"The thing that hurt most was to see him get discouraged. His ultimate goal was so near, yet so far away. It wasn't really that he was doing things wrong, but that he wasn't doing them the way he had done before. Sometimes he'd stand out there just as though he were on the sidelines, not wanting to get involved with the play. And there were times he wondered if he'd ever make it back.

"When he was sure he had lost a game, he would sometimes get very emotional, calling himself a liability to the team. And more than once he said, 'If I can't shake this mental block I'll never make it.' But now he's starting to hit opposing players, and he's going into the corners more.

"I went to every home game I could," Pat went on. "I'd drive in with a friend who met her husband at the game, and then Teddy and I would return home together. I got so I could tell how well he'd do just by watching him after the first two shifts. He often started shaky, but recovered. If he continued shaky on the third shift, I knew it would be a bad night. If he didn't, it would be a good one.

"Hockey wives get to know the game because they live with it. I'm no expert, but I know the requirements of Teddy's job and when he's fulfilling them. When he played poorly, all I could do was point out the things he had done well. Still, I suffered with Teddy whenever he missed a block or failed to check a man or lost control of the puck.

"I knew he didn't want to take those bad games home with him, but he had to talk about them. Most of the time I let him talk, because I thought it was good for him to get it out of his system. But sometimes he was so terribly down I felt I had to encourage him—to look at the good side instead of the bad. And I often reminded him that his progress had been much faster than anyone—including me—had anticipated.

"But Teddy didn't want to accept the good when there was anything bad. He wanted to get everything back at once, and couldn't understand why he made so many mistakes. There was no way I could convince him that he performed a miracle every time he went on the ice."

Despite my generally poor play at the time, I scored two goals in the latter part of October, both before home crowds at the Boston Garden. For the first, against Philadelphia on the 25th, I was close to the Flyers' goal and slapped in a rebound. It happened so fast I didn't realize for a second that I actually had scored and that the crowd was going crazy—yelling my name, cheering, clapping, really raising the roof. I wanted to do something to show my appreciation, but couldn't think of anything as I skated back to my position with a big grin on my face.

Six nights later, on the 31st, I scored another, this time against the Rangers in Boston. It was a better goal than the first one because I shot from farther out and was where I should have been. Once again the crowd went mad. They cheered and cheered, and that time I tipped my helmet. I guess it was the first time in NHL history that anyone did that, since most guys don't wear helmets.

I was involved in breaking a speed record for scoring three goals in 20 seconds on February 25 against Vancouver in Boston. Johnny Bucyk scored the first with assists from Phil Esposito and Johnny McKenzie. I passed to Eddie Westfall, who scored the second. And then I scored myself on a pass from Turk Sanderson. The old record had been set in 1952 when Johnny Mosienko of Chicago scored all three goals in 21 seconds.

From late February on, I was much more myself. At first I wasn't hitting guys, partly because I didn't think I was ready for it and partly because I didn't feel like hitting anyone. I purposely avoided contact. Later, however, I started giving good clean body checks, a defenseman's stock-in-trade. I got hit a few times, too. The opposition treated me with kid gloves early in the season, but that didn't last long. Some guys who would never have come near me before I was hurt were taking shots at me. Two I kept a mental book on. And when I got an opening in later games, I let them know that poor old Teddy Green was now quite able to handle himself.

After the Maloney fight in Chicago, I was less careful about avoiding contact. I'd learned I could still defend myself and still throw punches with my left. In Toronto on February 14, I got into a lovely battle with Brian Spencer in front of our net. It started as a punching match between us, then, remembering that it's the first blow that counts, I swung on him while keeping him tied up. Spencer didn't throw a punch. Later, I read that Spencer didn't swing because he was afraid of hurting me. This was so much baloney. He didn't swing because he couldn't. But I then realized there would be times when I'd be damned if I did and damned if I didn't. When I beat a guy in a fight, somebody would say the other guy felt sorry for me. Or when I didn't throw punches myself, somebody would say I didn't want to get hurt. Again, so much baloney.

I guess every hockey fan in Vancouver was wondering

what would happen when I first faced Wayne Maki, although nobody said much about it. We met in an afternoon game on October 18. Truly, I felt no different playing against him than against anyone else. When we first got out on the ice before the game began, Maki motioned me over to talk with him. When I paid no attention, he skated over and said he'd like to talk to me. But I refused, as I don't want to talk to him on or off the ice. I still think he took a cheap shot at me. And what good does talking about it do?

People wondered if I'd go after him, or if my teammates would. That didn't happen because they knew I didn't want them to. As for me, I checked Maki once in Vancouver—really barely brushed him—but stayed away from him altogether the next time the teams met. I'll probably always try to stay away from him. The reason is that to this day a lot of people are just waiting for me to make a big issue of it. I don't want to give anyone something to talk about when it pains me even to think about it.

The only time I have ever been involved in a stick fight was when I was provoked by a stick. It's true I don't hesitate to fight. But I always drop my gloves and stick, as I did in the Maloney fight and in the few other fights I got into during the 1970–71 season. But the Maki episode actually started when he speared me with his stick and I retaliated with mine. Except I don't think I shall ever do so again. I realize now, more than anyone else in the NHL, what can happen.

I look to the future with hope and happiness. Considering all things, I had a good season. The Boston fans gave me a night at the Garden that Pat and I will never forget—not just a Teddy Green night, but a night for the whole Green family. And the warmth and understanding of the fans, who bore with me through some bad games and overlooked some bad play, will stay with us forever.

On my night in Boston, I was showered with gifts. Including a silver plate from the Montreal team, our opponents that evening. But when I stepped before the microphone to try to express my thanks, all the emotions of the past year rushed together to form a lump in my throat. So I couldn't speak for a moment.

Just then a voice called out from the balcony. "That's okay, Teddy, we love you anyway!" It was a fan. A friend.

I was back home again.